THE SHOOTING SCRIPT

LITTLE MISS SUNSHINE

THE SHOOTING SCRIPT

LITTLE MISS SUNSHINE

SCREENPLAY AND NOTES BY
MICHAEL ARNDT

FOREWORD BY
DIRECTORS JONATHAN DAYTON AND VALERIE FARIS

newmarket press
for itbooks
AN IMPRINT OF HARPERCOLLINS PUBLISHERS

A Newmarket Shooting Script® Series Book

The Newmarket Shooting Script® Series is a registered trademark.

Copyright © 2006 Twentieth Century Fox Film Corporation. Foreword copyright © 2007 by Jonathan Dayton and Valerie Faris. Introduction copyright © 2007 by Michael Arndt.

First Newmarket Press for It Books edition published 2012.

10 9 8 7 6 5 4

ISBN 978-1-55704-770-0

Library of Congress Catalog-in-Publication Data available upon request.

OTHER BOOKS IN THE NEWMARKET SHOOTING SCRIPT® SERIES INCLUDE:

OTHER NEWMARKET PICTORIAL MOVIEBOOKS AND NEWMARKET INSIDER FILM BOOKS INCLUDE:

*Includes Screenplay

CONTENTS

CONTENTS

FOREWORD

We are somewhat of an oddity in this business. We are a directing *team,* we're *married,* and we have three *children.* The question we have been asked in nearly every interview is, "How do you direct together?" We say it's a lot like parenting, just much easier. But also like parenting, you work together with a mutual love for something outside yourself. So we suppose you could say the key ingredient is love. We could not raise a child we didn't love, and the same goes for making a film. Well, at least that is the way we justify the many years it took us to find the right film to make.

Thankfully Michael Arndt wrote *Little Miss Sunshine.* Luckily we got to read it and feel with absolute certainty that this was the film for us. No convincing yourself it's the right thing to do, no pressures from the outside, just the desire and the passion to realize something you wholeheartedly believe in.

Michael, we are forever indebted to you for allowing us to raise your baby.

—Jonathan Dayton and Valerie Faris

As for happiness, it is really useful to us in one way only, by making unhappiness possible. It is necessary for us to form in happiness ties of confidence and attachment that are both sweet and strong in order that their rupture may cause us the heart-rending but so valuable agony that is called unhappiness. Had we not been happy, if only in hope, the unhappiness that befalls us would be without cruelty and therefore without fruit. . . . The happy years are the lost, the wasted years, one must wait for suffering before one can work.
                                                              —Marcel Proust

If there's one thing in this world I hate, it's losers. I despise them.
                                                              —Arnold Schwarzenegger

INTRODUCTION

WINNING, LOSING, AND *LITTLE MISS SUNSHINE*

Part of the romance of movies—one of the elemental myths of show biz—is their ability to transform lives seemingly overnight ("You're going out there a nobody, kid, but you're coming back a star!"). That has been, to some degree, my story: I wrote *Little Miss Sunshine* when I was unemployed, living in a small one-bedroom walk-up in Brooklyn, and slowly burning through my hard-earned savings. I had quit my job and given myself a year off, hoping to write a salable script in that time. It was the financial equivalent of jumping off a cliff and trying to build an airplane on the way down. I had never made a dime from creative writing. I had no credits, no agent, no publishing history.

I was—in every external—a complete and total loser.

What I did have, though, was an enormous sense of happiness and purpose (finally, I could write full-time!) and a boundless, delusional self-confidence. I spent a year writing and, with my bank balance dipping into negative territory, gave one of my scripts, *Little Miss Sunshine,* to my friend Karyn Kusama, who had just directed the film *Girlfight*. She read the script, liked it, and passed it along to her agent, Tom Strickler of the Endeavor Agency.

I waited. Days turned into weeks. My boundless and delusional confidence began to falter. I started, for the first time, to contemplate the prospect of failure. I had worked very hard, for many years, trying to learn the craft of screenwriting, and had written what I felt was the best script I could write. What if nothing came of it?

For one unhappy week, I considered whether I should do something else with my life. What I was trying to do—write an original screenplay that would be bought and turned into a movie—suddenly seemed impossible. It would never happen. Not, at least, to me.

In the end, I decided to forge ahead—I'd get another day job and continue writing. I'd try to shoot *Little Miss Sunshine* as a no-budget DV feature. I loved movies, and there was nothing else I wanted to do with my life. Still, the sting of failure was as painful as anything I'd ever experienced, and it left me, I would say, permanently humbled.

The story, of course, has a happy ending. At the end of that week I got a message on my machine from Tom saying he'd read my script and "really liked it, actually." Five months later, the script was sold for more money than I'd made in the rest of my life combined.

A Chronology:

On Tuesday, May 23, 2000, at 4:27 p.m., I sat down to write LMS. I wrote twelve pages the first day, thirty-seven pages the second, and—pulling an all-nighter—fifty-four pages on the third day. I finished the first draft at 9:56 a.m. on Friday, May 26.

Then I spent a year rewriting it.

On July 29, 2001—a Sunday—I heard from Tom Strickler.

On December 21, 2001—the Friday before the holidays—the script was purchased by producer Marc Turtletaub.

Principal photography began on June 6, 2005, and ended—after thirty shooting days—on July 18.

The film had its world premiere on January 20, 2006, at Sundance, and was bought by Fox Searchlight the next day.

Little Miss Sunshine opened in theaters on July 26, 2006.

As of this writing (November 6, 2006), it has grossed $75 million worldwide.

So the film has "succeeded," and I have (temporarily, at least) escaped from the jaws of failure.

In many ways, though, my life has remained much as it was in 2000. I still rent the same one-bedroom walk-up in Brooklyn, and I still spend my days sitting in a chair and staring at a computer (though the chair is more comfortable and the computer is nicer). The main difference is I don't worry about having to get a day job. (Not yet, anyway.)

A number of people who know my story have been quick to seize upon it as a rewards-of-virtue narrative—all that effort and persistence, they tell me, was bound to pay off. In this view of the world, character is destiny and success is the logical—almost inevitable—consequence of hard work, patience, and a shrewdly applied intelligence.

That is not how I see things.

From my perspective, the difference between success and failure was razor-thin and depended—to a terrifying degree—upon chance, serendipity, and all manner of things beyond my control. A thousand things could have gone wrong in the five years it took to turn *Little Miss Sunshine* into a movie, any one of which could have destroyed the project.

Yet at every turn the script was met with good fortune; every setback was revealed to be a blessing in disguise. I was lucky to stumble upon the right agents, who got it to the right producers, who chose the right directors, who cast (perfectly) the right actors and hired the right crew. A single misstep in this concatenation and the film would have been made badly or, more likely, not at all.

Which brings me—in a roundabout way—to Richard Hoover, Winning and Losing, and the underlying concerns of *Little Miss Sunshine*.

All of us lead two lives—our public lives, which are visible to others, and our private lives, which are not. Richard is obsessed with the values of public life—status, rank, "success." His view of the world, divided into Winners and Losers, judges everyone—including himself—accordingly. These values have become seemingly inescapable in our media-saturated culture—from *American Idol,* to professional sports, to the weekend box office reports. Everything, it seems, has become a contest.

The problem with this worldview is that it neglects and devalues the realm of the private—family, friendship, romance, childhood, pleasure, imagination, and the concerns of the spirit. Our private lives—invisible to the outside world—tend to be far richer and more gratifying than the rewards of public life. We would do well, as poets and philosophers have long advised, to turn away from the bustle of the world and cultivate the gardens of our souls.

And yet—as I learned in July 2001—it is extremely difficult to set aside the judgments of the world and march to your own drummer. To "do what you love and fuck the rest," as Dwayne says. That is a hard path, and not often one that leads to happiness or fulfillment (see van Gogh's letters). I wouldn't recommend it to everyone.

What I would recommend—and this is the central hope of the movie—is that we make an effort to judge our lives and the lives of others according to our own criteria, distinct from the facile and shallow judgments of the marketplace.

James Joyce once said we should treat both success and failure as the impostors they are. I would humbly concur—the real substance of life is elsewhere.

—Michael Arndt

Little Miss Sunshine

By

Michael Arndt

Shooting Script - 5/09/05
Blue Revisions   - 5/17/05
Pink Revisions   - 5/20/05
Green Revisions - 5/31/05
Yellow Revisions - 6/02/05
Goldenrod Revs. - 6/06/05

1   ECU - VIDEO PIXELS

Five young women stand side by side, waiting to be judged --
breathless, hopeful. A name is announced. Four hearts break.

The camera ZOOMS across the smiles of the losers to find a winner.
She bursts into tears, hugs the nearest runner up.

Begin CREDITS. MUSIC -- quiet and melancholy -- plays over
all the opening scenes, leading to the Title card.

The Contest Winner cries and hugs the Runners-up as she has the
tiara pinned on her head. Then -- carrying her bouquet -- she
strolls down the runway, waving and blowing kisses.

2   INT. BASEMENT REC ROOM - DAY   2

A seven-year-old girl sits watching the show intently.

This is OLIVE. She is big for her age and slightly plump.

She has frizzy hair and wears black-rimmed glasses. She
studies the show very earnestly.

Then, using a remote, she FREEZES the image.

Absently, she holds up one hand and mimics the waving style
of Miss America. She REWINDS the tape and starts all over.

Again, Miss America hears her name announced, and once again
breaks down in tears -- overwhelmed and triumphant.

                         RICHARD (V.O.)
                There's two kinds of people in this
                world -- Winners...and Losers.

3   INT. CLASSROOM - DAY   3

RICHARD (45) stands at the front of a generic community
college classroom -- cinderblock walls, industrial carpeting.

He wears pleated khaki shorts, a golf shirt, sneakers. He
moves with the stocky, stiff-legged gait of a former athlete.

His peppy, upbeat demeanor just barely masks a seething sense
of insecurity and frustration. MUSIC continues underneath.

                         RICHARD
                If there's one thing you take away from
                the nine weeks we've spent here, it should
                be this: Winners and Losers. What's the
                difference?

Richard turns and clicks through a Power Point presentation,
projected behind him, that bullet-lists his key points.

                    RICHARD (cont'd)
          Winners see their dreams come true.
          Winners see what they want, they go out and
          they get it. They don't hesitate. They
          don't complain. They don't make excuses.
          And they <u>don't</u> give up. Losers don't get
          what they want. They hesitate. They
          complain. They make excuses. And they
          give up. On themselves and their dreams.

Richard puts down his remote for the big finale. In the dim
half-light, it's a hushed, dramatic moment.

                    RICHARD (cont'd)
          Inside each of you -- at the very core
          of your being -- is a Winner waiting to
          be awakened...and unleashed upon the
          world. With my Nine Step "Refuse To
          Lose" program, you now have the tools,
          the know-how, the insights you need to
          put your losing habits behind you and
          <u>make</u> your dreams come true. No
          hesitating! No complaining! No
          excuses! I want you to go out into the
          world...and be Winners! Thank you!

Big smile.

REVERSE ANGLE -- There are twenty STUDENTS in a classroom
that could seat one hundred. They CLAP half-heartedly.

Then there's an awkward moment when everyone gathers their
stuff. No one says anything. Chairs SCRAPE the floor.

4   INT. DWAYNE'S BEDROOM - DAY   4

DWAYNE is a handsome, skinny fifteen year old. He lies on
his back in his bedroom, bench-pressing a barbell.

The bedroom is dominated by a huge portrait of Friedrich
Nietzsche, painted on a bed sheet, hanging on one wall.

                                                   JUMP CUTS:

Dwayne does vertical sit-ups on a wall-mounted brace.

Dwayne does vertical push-ups leaning against the wall.

Dwayne breathes heavily, having finished his work-out.

He walks to a home-made calender on the wall made from a long
roll of computer paper. It is marked, "Enlistment."

On the roll is a long grid of maybe a thousand squares.
About half the squares have been filled in with magic marker.

Dwayne uncaps a magic marker and fills in one more square.

5   INT. BATHROOM - DAY   5

Two hands spill a brown powder onto a small mirror.

A razor blade cuts the powder into lines.

A rolled-up dollar bill lowers. The lines are snorted.

The snorter lifts his head up. He is a short, chunky,
balding old man -- a Roz Chast kind of grandfather.

This is GRANDPA, 80 years old.

He sits down on the toilet seat, rubs his nose, takes a
breath and relaxes as the drugs flood his system.

                    SHERYL (V.O.)
          ...Yeah, I'm on my way.

6   INT. CAR - DAY   6

A woman, SHERYL, 40s, is smoking and talking on a cell phone
as she weaves through a strip-mall landscape. She wears
office attire and a name tag that reads, "Sheryl Hoover,
Senior Account Manager".

                    SHERYL
          ...I don't know how long... I
          don't know...! Richard, he doesn't
          have anywhere else to go!

She takes a drag, listens with increasing irritation, then
exhales. A beat.

                    SHERYL (cont'd)
          I'm not smoking... I'm not! Look,
          I'm at the hospital... Okay, bye.

She beeps off her phone.

7   EXT. HOSPITAL CORRIDOR - DAY   7

Sheryl strides anxiously down a hospital corridor, fingering a small
cross on her necklace, checking room numbers. She finds the room
she's looking for. As she tries to enter, a DOCTOR emerges. They
nearly collide.

                    DOCTOR
          Ms. Hoover?
               (Sheryl nods)
          Your brother's fine...

Sheryl exhales -- hugely relieved.

8   INT. HOSPITAL ROOM - DAY   8

In a wheelchair, parked against a wall, is Sheryl's brother, FRANK, also middle-aged. His wrists are wrapped in bandages.

With empty eyes, he listens to the muted VOICE of the Doctor coming from the hallway.

> DOCTOR (O.S.)
> ...Keep him away from sharp objects: knives, scissors... If you have medications -- depressants -- in your house, keep them secured...

9   INT. HOSPITAL CORRIDOR - DAY   9

Sheryl listens to the Doctor.

> DOCTOR
> I'd prefer to keep him, but...

> SHERYL
> I know, the insurance...

She shakes her head and sighs.

> DOCTOR
> You want to see him...?

10   INT. HOSPITAL ROOM - DAY   10

Sheryl and the Doctor enter. Frank barely reacts.

> SHERYL
> Hey, Frank...

> FRANK
> Sheryl.

Fighting tears, she goes and hugs him.

> SHERYL
> I'm so glad you're still here.

> FRANK
> Well. That's one of us.

11   INT. CAR - DAY   11

Sheryl drives Frank home from the hospital. They say nothing. Sheryl sneaks glances at Frank. Hesitantly:

> SHERYL
> You want to talk? Or no?

Frank stares at the road in front of them. Finally:

                    FRANK
          No.

                    SHERYL
          Okay.

She nods. They keep driving.

                                        FADE TO BLACK

TITLE: "LITTLE MISS SUNSHINE"

MUSIC ENDS. FADE IN a phone RINGING.

12   INT. KITCHEN, OFFICE - DAY   12

An empty kitchen. A phone and answering machine sit in the
FOREGROUND. On the third RING, the machine picks up.

                    SHERYL (O.C.)
                    (filtered)
          You've reached the Hoover
          residence. We're sorry we can't
          take your call right now. Please
          leave a message.

BEEEP. An excited female voice, CINDY. In the background,
two young GIRLS chime in, ad-libbing congratulations: "Yay,
Olive!"; "We knew you could do it!"; "Whooooo-hooooo!"

                    CINDY (O.C.)
                    (filtered)
          Sheryl, it's Cindy! Listen, this
          is so great! Remember when Olive
          was here last month, she was runner
          up in the regional Little Miss
          Sunshine? Well, they just called
          right now and said that the girl
          who won had to forfeit her crown.
          I don't know why -- something about
          diet pills -- but anyway, that
          means Olive won the regionals! So
          now she has a place in the State
          contest in Redondo Beach! They
          want to make sure she can make it,
          so you gotta call right away. The
          woman's name is Nancy Jenkins and
          her number...

BEEEEP. The machine cuts him off.

In the background, through a doorway, the front door opens.
Sheryl and Frank enter carrying several bags and suitcases.

6.

                          SHERYL
                      (calling out)
                  Hello! Anyone...?!

13   INT. HALLWAY - DAY   13

      She leads Frank down a hallway. He follows passively.

                          SHERYL
                  Down here. We have you with Dwayne.

      She knocks and pushes open the door to Dwayne's room. Dwayne
      is on the bed, reading THUS SPOKE ZARATHUSTRA. He sits up.

                          SHERYL (cont'd)
                  Dwayne? Hi, Uncle Frank's here.

      Frank hesitates. He gives Sheryl a look: "You're kidding."

                          SHERYL (cont'd)
                  He doesn't mind, Frank. We talked.

      Frank makes a half-gesture towards the rest of the house.

                          SHERYL (cont'd)
                  We can't have you sleeping alone.
                  The doctors said...
                      (he looks at her)
                  I'm sorry. I have to insist.

      Dwayne gets up and exits the room, pushing past them and
      avoiding eye contact. Sheryl enters the bedroom.

14   INT. DWAYNE'S BEDROOM - DAY   14

      Sheryl goes and brushes off a cot. Frank remains outside.

                          SHERYL
                  You'll get along fine. He's really
                  quiet. Look, I set up a cot.
                      (he hesitates)
                  Please, Frank? Please?

      Very unhappily, Frank enters the room and just stands there.

                          SHERYL (cont'd)
                  Thank you. I gotta start dinner.
                  Come out when you're settled? And
                  leave the door open. That's
                  important.
                      (beat)
                  I'm glad you're here.

      She gives him a kiss on the cheek, then departs.

Frank sits on the cot in his nephew's bedroom. On it is a
Muppet sleeping bag with the Cookie Monster eating a cookie.
Frank glances at the sleeping bag, then averts his eyes.

This is pretty much the worst moment of his life.

15   INT. DINING ROOM - DAY   15

Dwayne is at the dinner table, reading. Sheryl walks by.

                    SHERYL
          Dwayne, honey, there's a bucket of
          chicken in the car. Can you get it
          and I'll make a salad?

Dwayne nods and silently gets up but -- entranced by the book
-- he keeps reading, trying to get to the end of the chapter.
Sheryl opens the door to the downstairs rec room and shouts.

                    SHERYL (cont'd)
          Olive?!

                    OLIVE (O.S.)
          Yeah?!

                    SHERYL
          Is Grandpa with you?!

                    OLIVE (O.S.)
          Yeah!

                    SHERYL
          What are you guys doing?

                    OLIVE (O.S.)
          Rehearsing!

                    SHERYL
          Okay! Dinner in ten minutes!

                    OLIVE (O.S.)
          Okay!

16   INT. KITCHEN - DAY   16

Sheryl enters, opens the refrigerator, and begins pulling out
stuff to make a salad.

Abruptly, from the kitchen side door, Richard enters.

                    RICHARD
          Hi.

                    SHERYL
          Hi. Frank's here.

                              RICHARD
                Oh. Did Stan Grossman call?

                              SHERYL
                Check the machine.

He walks over and hits the answering machine.

                              MACHINE
                Hello. You have one message.

It rewinds. Sheryl calls to Dwayne, still reading.

                              SHERYL
                Dwayne...?! The chicken? Please?
                It's in the car. And can you set
                the table? We'll just do paper
                plates tonight.

Dwayne snaps the paperback closed and departs. Sheryl pulls
off her business-wear jacket and exits in the other
direction. The phone message begins.

                              CINDY (O.C.)
                         (filtered)
                Sheryl, it's Cindy! Listen, this
                is so great! Remember when Olive
                was here last month, she was runner
                up in the regional Little Miss
                Sunshine?

                              RICHARD
                         (calling to Sheryl)
                It's from your sister!
                         (to himself)
                Fuck!

He STOPS the message, picks up the phone and dials. Sheryl
re-enters, pulling on a sweatshirt, and returns to making her
salad. Over the following, Dwayne comes in and out, picking
up stuff to set the table.

Richard takes a breath and assumes an office-voice.

                              RICHARD (cont'd)
                         (into phone)
                Richard Hoover for Stan Grossman.
                Can you reach him? Yeah, tell him
                I want to know this thing is done.
                No, I understand that. I
                understand.
                         (rolls his eyes)
                              (MORE)

                         RICHARD (cont'd)
          Look -- he has my cell, if he could
          just call me anytime over the
          weekend and let me know we're on,
          I'd be very, very grateful. Okay.
          Thank you. Bye.

He hangs up.

                         RICHARD (cont'd)
          Bitch.

                         SHERYL
          Richard...! So what happened with
          Stan Grossman?

                         RICHARD
          He's still in Scottsdale.

                         SHERYL
          So why hasn't he called?

                         RICHARD
          Will you let me worry about this?!

Sheryl exhales, goes back to her salad. Dwayne comes in.

                         SHERYL
          Dwayne, can you check on Frank?
          Tell him it's dinner time.

Dwayne nods and heads off. Sheryl walks back to the door to
the downstairs rec room and opens it again.

                         SHERYL (cont'd)
          Olive?! Dinner time!

                         OLIVE (O.S.)
          Okay!

17   INT. DWAYNE'S BEDROOM - DAY   17

Frank sits on the cot, staring at the floor. FOOTSTEPS approach.

Dwayne appears in the door, knocks. He mimes eating.

                         FRANK
          Dinner?
               (Dwayne nods)
          What? You don't talk anymore?
               (Dwayne shakes his head)
          Why not?

Dwayne rolls his eyes and half-shrugs.

                         FRANK (cont'd)
          You _can_ talk. You just choose not to?

Dwayne nods. Then he points to the bed-sheet painting of
Nietzsche hanging on his wall. Frank turns and looks.

>   FRANK (cont'd)
>   Is that Nietzsche? You don't speak
>   because of Friedrich Nietzsche?

Dwayne nods, turns and leaves. Frank considers this.

>   FRANK (cont'd)
>   Far out.

18   INT. DINING ROOM - DAY   18

Dwayne sits in his chair, folds his arms, and -- scowling -- waits
for everyone else to arrive. Frank tentatively follows. Sheryl
comes out and puts her salad on the table.

>   SHERYL
>   Frank, you can sit here, next to
>   Dwayne. Here's the salad. I'm
>   gonna run get Sprite for everyone.

She walks off, pausing to open the rec room door again.

>   SHERYL (cont'd)
>   Olive! Come on! Dinner time!

>   OLIVE (O.S.)
>   Coming!!!

Sheryl disappears, leaving Dwayne and Frank alone. Frank
sits. Dwayne scowls at the table in front of him.

Frank looks at his place setting -- a paper plate and a Big
Gulp cup with the Incredible Hulk on it. He picks up the cup
and examines it dispassionately. He puts it down.

Dwayne doesn't move. Frank glances at Dwayne, not knowing
what to do. He seems to have met someone who is at least as
unhappy as he is. This intrigues him. He ventures:

>   FRANK
>   Got a girlfriend?

Dwayne looks at Frank, then shakes his head.

>   FRANK (cont'd)
>   Boyfriend?

Dwayne gives Frank a look.

                    FRANK (cont'd)
         Kidding. Kidding. I know.
              (beat)
         So who do you hang out with?

Dwayne shakes his head.

                    FRANK (cont'd)
         No one? There must be someone...!
              (Dwayne shakes his head)
         You don't hang out with anyone? Oh
         come on. You must have <u>one</u> friend!

Dwayne reaches in his shirt pocket and pulls out a palm-sized
pad of paper. He flips it open and scribbles a note.

He shows it to Frank. It reads:

              "I hate everyone."

                    FRANK (cont'd)
         Everyone? What about your family?

Dwayne scribbles again. He shows it to Frank. It now reads:

              "<u>I hate everyone</u>!!!"

He's underlined "everyone" three times. Frank looks at him.

                    FRANK (cont'd)
         You hate me?

Dwayne considers this. He scribbles a new note. It reads:

              "Not yet."

                    FRANK (cont'd)
         Fair enough.

They go back to sitting in silence. Richard comes out.

                    RICHARD
         Frank. Good to see you.

                    FRANK
         Richard...

They shake. Richard sits down. Silence. Richard stands up.

                    RICHARD
         I'm gonna get Olive.

He walks to the downstairs doorway and shouts.

                         RICHARD (cont'd)
          Dad! Olive! Come on!

                         OLIVE (O.S.)
               (shrieking)
          We're coming!!!

Sheryl enters with a big bottle of Diet Sprite.

                         SHERYL
          You guys, go on and start. Frank,
          some Sprite? I want everyone to
          have at least a little salad.

                         FRANK
          Thanks, Sheryl.

She pours him a cup, sits down, and starts opening containers
of cole slaw and mashed potatoes.

Richard returns to the table, sits, and grabs a piece of
chicken from the bucket. Dwayne follows suit, as does Frank.

The meal begins. Three seconds of silence.

                         FRANK (cont'd)
          So, Sheryl... I couldn't help
          noticing Dwayne has stopped speaking.

                         SHERYL
          Oh! I'm sorry. Dwayne's taken a
          vow of silence.

                         FRANK
          You've taken a vow of silence?!

Dwayne nods.

                         SHERYL
          He's gonna join the Air Force
          Academy and become a test pilot.
          He's taken a vow of silence until
          he reaches that goal.

                         FRANK
               (to Dwayne)
          You're kidding...!

Dwayne stares at Frank. He's not kidding. Olive enters the dining
room, with Grandpa following.

                         OLIVE
          Hi, Uncle Frank!

                    FRANK
          Olive. Boy, you're gettin' big! You're
          like a real person now!

Olive, unprompted, walks over and gives him a kiss on the
cheek. She sees the bandages on Frank's wrists.

                    OLIVE
          What happened to your arms?

                    SHERYL
          Olive...

                    FRANK
          No, it's okay. I had a little
          accident. I'm okay now.

                    RICHARD
          How's the new routine coming?

                    OLIVE
          It's good.

                    RICHARD
          When're you gonna let us see it?

                    OLIVE
          I dunno. It's up to Grandpa.

                    GRANDPA
          A couple of days. It still needs work.

Olive sits. Grandpa walks to the table.

                    GRANDPA (cont'd)
          What is this?! Chicken?! Every
          day it's the fucking chicken! Holy
          God almighty! Is it possible, just
          one time, we could have something
          for dinner except the goddamn
          fucking chicken?!

Sheryl ignores him. Richard tries to cut him off.

                    RICHARD
          Dad... Dad... Dad... Dad!!!

                    GRANDPA
          I'm just saying...!

                    RICHARD
          If you want to buy your own food,
          you're more than welcome...

                          GRANDPA
          Christ. Y'know, at Sunset Manor...

                          RICHARD
          If you liked Sunset Manor so much
          maybe you shouldn't have gotten
          yourself kicked out of there...!

                          GRANDPA
                    (waves dismissively)
          Ahhhh...!

He takes out a piece of chicken and starts eating. A tense
silence. Frank tries to get things going again.

                          FRANK
          When did you start? With the vow?

Dwayne shrugs. He doesn't care to comment.

                          RICHARD
          It's been nine months. He hasn't
          said a word. I think it shows
          tremendous discipline.

                          SHERYL
          Richard...

                          RICHARD
          I'm serious! I think we could all learn
          something from what Dwayne's doing!
          Dwayne has a goal. He has a dream. It
          may not be my dream, or your dream, but
          still... He's pursuing that dream with
          focus and discipline. In fact, I was
          thinking about the Nine Steps...

                          GRANDPA
          Oh, for crying out loud...!

                          RICHARD
                    (evenly)
          ...About the Nine Steps, and how
          Dwayne's utilizing at least seven
          of them in his journey to personal
          fulfillment.

                          SHERYL
          Richard. Please.

                          RICHARD
          I'm just saying! I've come around! I
          think Dwayne deserves our support.

Frank looks at Dwayne. Dwayne rolls his eyes. Olive
addresses Frank.

>   OLIVE
>   How did it happen?

>   FRANK
>   How did what happen?

>   OLIVE
>   Your accident...

>   SHERYL
>   Honey...

She shakes her head: "Don't go there."

>   FRANK
>   No, it's okay. Unless you object...

>   SHERYL
>   No, I'm pro-honesty here. I just
>   think, you know... It's up to you.

>   FRANK
>   Be my guest...

>   SHERYL
>   Olive, Uncle Frank didn't really
>   have an accident. What happened
>   was: he tried to kill himself.

>   OLIVE
>   You did? Why?

>   RICHARD
>   I don't think this is an
>   appropriate conversation.
>   (to Olive)
>   Let's leave Uncle Frank alone.

A beat. Olive has stopped eating.

>   OLIVE
>   Why did you want to kill yourself?

>   RICHARD
>   Frank. Don't answer that question.

Frank stares at Richard. He turns back to Olive.

>   FRANK
>   I tried to kill myself because I
>   was very unhappy.

                         RICHARD
                       (overlapping)
          Don't listen, honey, he's sick and
          he doesn't know what he's...

                         SHERYL
          Richard... Richard... Richard...

                         RICHARD
          What?! I don't think it's
          appropriate for a seven year old!

                         SHERYL
          She's gonna find out anyway. Go
          on, Frank.

                         OLIVE
          Why were you unhappy?

Frank glances at Richard -- deadpan victorious -- and
continues.

                         FRANK
          Well, there were a lot of reasons.
          Mainly, though, I fell in love with
          someone who didn't love me back...

                         OLIVE
          Who?

                         FRANK
          One of my grad students. I was
          very much in love with him.

                         OLIVE
          Him? It was a boy? You fell in
          love with a boy?

                         FRANK
          Yes. I did. Very much so.

This is new to Olive. She thinks it over.

                         OLIVE
          That's silly.

                         FRANK
          You're right. It was very, very
          silly.

                         GRANDPA
          There's another word for it...

                         RICHARD
          Dad...

                    OLIVE
          So... That's when you tried to
          kill yourself...?

                    FRANK
          Well, no. What happened was: the
          boy I was in love with fell in love
          with another man, Larry Sugarman.

                    SHERYL
          Who's Larry Sugarman?

                    FRANK
          Larry Sugarman is perhaps the
          second most highly regarded Proust
          scholar in the U.S.

                    RICHARD
          Who's number one?

                    FRANK
          That would be me, Rich.

                    OLIVE
          So... That's when you tried...?

                    FRANK
          Well, no. What happened was: I was a bit
          upset. I said some things I shouldn't
          have said. I did some things I shouldn't
          have done. And subsequently, I was fired
          from my job, forced to give up my
          apartment and move into a motel.

                    OLIVE
          Oh. So that's when...?

                    FRANK
                (hesitates)
          Well, no. Actually, all that was
          okay. What happened was: two days
          ago the MacArthur Foundation -- in
          its infinite wisdom -- decided to
          award a "genius" grant to Larry
          Sugarman.
                (deep breath)
          And that's when...

                    GRANDPA
          ...You tried to check out early.

                    FRANK
          Yes. And I failed at that as well.

                              RICHARD
                    Olive, what's important to
                    understand is that Uncle Frank gave
                    up on himself. He made a series of
                    foolish choices, and then he gave
                    up on himself, which is something
                    that winners never do.

A beat. Frank looks like he could leap across the table and
strangle Richard. Sheryl intervenes.

                              SHERYL
                    So that's the story, okay? Let's
                    move on. Olive, how's your new
                    routine coming?

                              OLIVE
                    Fine. I told you.

Over the above, Frank turns and asks, regarding Richard:

                              FRANK
                    Is he always like this?
                              (Dwayne nods)
                    How can you stand it?

Dwayne writes a note, shows it to Frank. It reads:

                    "I can't."

Frank nods. Richard addresses Olive.

                              RICHARD
                    Honey, tell Frank why you're doing
                    your dance routine.

                              FRANK
                    Olive. Why are you doing a dance
                    routine?

                              OLIVE
                    For Little Miss Chili Pepper.

                              FRANK
                              (arch)
                    A-ha! Just as I suspected...!

                              SHERYL
                    Olive, tell him what Little Miss
                    Chili Pepper is.

                              OLIVE
                    Little Miss Chili Pepper is a beauty
                    contest for everyone in Albuquerque.
                              (MORE)

                    OLIVE (cont'd)
          But you have to be six or seven years old
          and you have to be a girl.

Frank looks skeptically at Sheryl.

                    SHERYL
          This is our sister.

                    FRANK
          Cindy.

                    SHERYL
                (nods)
          She got Olive hooked in California.

Frank rolls his eyes, understanding. He turns back to Olive.

                    FRANK
          So what do you think your chances are?

Olive takes the question like a pro.

                    OLIVE
          I think I can win. Because some of
          the other girls? Have been doing it
          longer? But I practice every day.

                    FRANK
          Well, good luck.

                    RICHARD
          It's not about luck. Luck is the
          name that losers give to their own
          failings. It's about wanting to
          win. Willing yourself to win. You
          got to want it badder than anyone.

                    OLIVE
          I do!

                    RICHARD
          Do you? Really?
                (a beat; she nods)
          Then you're gonna be a winner!

She smiles. Dwayne shakes his head and keeps eating.

                    SHERYL
          Richard...

                    RICHARD
          What?! It's true!

                    OLIVE
          I was runner up in California!

FRANK
When were you in California?

SHERYL
Spring break. Dwayne went to visit
his Dad in Florida for two weeks.
Olive went out to see her cousins
in Laguna. She made it to the top
of the Regionals out there.

OLIVE
I was second place.

RICHARD
Sher, y'know, there's a message
from Cindy on the machine.

SHERYL
Yeah. Did you hear what it was?

RICHARD
Actually, it was something about
Little Miss Sunshine.

OLIVE
What? Little Miss Sunshine? What?!

She runs off. Sheryl follows Olive into the kitchen.

19   INT. KITCHEN, OFFICE - DAY   19

Sheryl and Olive approach the answering machine. The
"message" light is blinking. Sheryl hits it.

                    CINDY (O.C.)
                     (filtered)
              Sheryl, it's Cindy...

20   INT. DINING ROOM - DAY   20

Richard, Frank, Dwayne and Grandpa, eating, try to listen.

19.1 INT. KITCHEN, OFFICE - DAY   19.1

Olive and Sheryl listen.

                    CINDY (O.C.)
                     (filtered)
              ...Something about diet pills, but anyway
              that means that Olive won the regionals,
              so now she has a place in the State
              contest in Redondo Beach...

BEEEP. Over the above, Olive reacts with involuntary spasms
of shock, disbelief, and then pure, unadulterated euphoria.

She waits -- trembling -- to hear the whole message. When it
ends, she puts her hands to her temples:

                    OLIVE
          Aaahhhhhhh!!! Aaahhhhhhhhhhhhhh!!!
          Little Miss Sunshine! Little Miss
          Sunshine! Little Miss Sunshine!!!

She goes running out into the dining room.

                    OLIVE (O.S.)(cont'd)
          Little Miss Sunshine! Little Miss
          Sunshine! Little Miss Sunshine!!!

Sheryl closes her eyes, exhales.

                    SHERYL
          Fuck...!

She picks up the cordless phone, dials.

21   INT. DINING ROOM - DAY   21

Sheryl re-enters with the phone. Olive is rejoicing.

                    OLIVE
          I won! I won! I get to go to the
          Championship! Oh, God! Oh, my God!
                    (beat)
          I gotta pack! I gotta go pack!

She rushes off to the downstairs doorway and disappears.

                    RICHARD
          Wait, Olive, finish your dinner!

                    OLIVE (O.S.)
          I'm finished!

                    GRANDPA
          What happened?

                    SHERYL
          Apparently, the girl who won
          Regionals was disqualified. So
          Olive has her place in the Finals.

                    RICHARD
          When are they?

                    SHERYL
          I'm calling... Cindy! Yeah, we
          just got it... Yeah, she basically
          went crazy... No, I didn't get
          that, the machine cut you off.

She grabs Dwayne's pen and pad. She scribbles.

                    SHERYL (cont'd)
          Redondo Beach. This Sunday?! Are
          you guys going?
                    (listens, frowns)
          You can't put it off...? So where
          does that leave us? No, I
          understand that, Cindy!
                    (shakes her head, fuming)
          No, we just have to figure this
          out. No, I'll give this lady a
          call and we'll figure it out.
          Right. Okay, bye.

She hangs up, irked.

                    RICHARD
          It's Sunday? Can Jeff and Cindy
          take her?

                    SHERYL
                    (shakes her head)
          They're doing this equestrian thing
          in Santa Barbara.

                    RICHARD
          They do that crap every weekend...!

                    SHERYL
          It's the Nationals, okay? Caitlin
          and Chelsea have been training all
          year. They're taking both horses...
          It's a big deal, apparently.

Richard exhales, exasperated.

                    RICHARD
          So what about Olive?

They all look at each other.

22   INT. REC ROOM - DAY   22

We TRACK with Olive as she runs down the stairs and races
around, picking up clothes and shoes scattered about.

23   INT. KITCHEN - MOMENTS LATER   23

Sheryl enters carrying the bucket of chicken, the half-filled
containers of potato salad and slaw, and used paper plates.

Richard follows Sheryl. Grandpa follows Richard.

                         SHERYL
          I have to go. I promised Olive she
          could go if she made the finals.

                         RICHARD
          You promised?

                         GRANDPA
          I'm going.

                         RICHARD
          Wait a minute, Dad...

                         SHERYL
          We'll fly out, come back Monday.

Sheryl throws the plates in the garbage. Throughout the
following, she wraps the leftover chicken in Saran Wrap and
puts the chicken and other leftovers in the fridge.

                         RICHARD
          How're you gonna get around down there?

                         SHERYL
          We'll rent a car.

                         RICHARD
          And stay in a hotel?

                         SHERYL
          We can afford it...!

                         RICHARD
          Sheryl...! This is our seed money!

                         SHERYL
          Well, if I had a little help
          bringing it in, y'know?! It all
          goes to your Nine Steps...

                         RICHARD
          Honey... Honey... Honey...
                    (patient)
          As soon as I get the word from Stan, I
          will pay you back, we'll start generating
          revenue. But in the meantime...

Sheryl exhales, grits her teeth, shakes her head.

                         SHERYL
          Okay, we'll drive.

                         GRANDPA
          I'm not driving...

                         RICHARD
          In the Miata? How're you gonna fit
          Grandpa?

                         SHERYL
          Grandpa doesn't have to come.

                         GRANDPA
          What...?! I coached her! I showed
          her the moves! I have to be there!

                         RICHARD
          Why don't you take the VW?

                         SHERYL
          I can't drive a shift, Richard!
          I've tried, and I can't do it!

Having put away the leftovers, Sheryl opens the freezer and
pulls out a Jumbo Pak of popsicles.

                         SHERYL (cont'd)
          We'll fly there.

                         RICHARD
          We can't afford it.

                         SHERYL
          Well, that's what we're gonna do!
          Unless you have a better idea.

She slams the freezer door and heads for the dining room.

24   INT. DINING ROOM - CONTINUOUS   24

Sheryl enters. Richard and Grandpa follow. Frank and Dwayne
are finishing up. Sheryl tosses the popsicles on the table.

                         SHERYL
          Here. This is dessert.

She sits, rips open a popsicle and takes a bite. Silence.
Dwayne and Frank glance at each other, then tentatively take
popsicles for themselves. Richard takes a deep breath.

                         RICHARD
          Okay. I'll drive the bus.

                         GRANDPA
          No! I'll take her on a plane!

Everyone ignores Grandpa. Sheryl considers Richard's idea.

                         SHERYL
          What about Dwayne and Frank?

                    RICHARD
          They can stay here.

Dwayne and Frank look at each other.

                    SHERYL
          No, that won't work.

                    RICHARD
          Why not?

                    SHERYL
          Richard...! I was told explicitly
          I could not leave Frank by himself.
          No offense, Frank.

                    FRANK
          None taken.

                    RICHARD
          So Dwayne's here! They can look
          after each other!

                    SHERYL
          No, Richard... That's asking too
          much! If something happened...!

                    RICHARD
          Well, I guess we can't go then! I
          mean, unless we take Frank and Dwayne
          with us!

A pause. All eyes turn to Frank and Dwayne. Dwayne begins
vigorously shaking his head "No".

25   INT. OLIVE'S BEDROOM - DAY   25

Olive enters with dresses, shoes, a swimsuit. She pulls a
suitcase from under her bed, and begins stuffing things in.

26   INT. DINING ROOM - DAY   26

Sheryl pleads with Frank and Dwayne.

                    SHERYL
          Frank?

Frank has a pained expression on his face. It's like he's
giving birth to this answer -- forcing it out of himself:

                    FRANK
          O-kay.

                    SHERYL
          Dwayne, please. For your sister?

                    RICHARD
         Come on, Dwayne! It'll be fun!

Everyone stares at him. Dwayne takes his pad out and writes.
Frank reads over his shoulder as it comes out.

                    FRANK
         "This...is...unfair...All...I...
         ask...is...that...you...leave...
         me...alone."

Dwayne stops writing, folds his arms. Silence. Off-screen,
we HEAR Olive packing. Sheryl turns to Dwayne.

                    SHERYL
         Dwayne: Flight school. I'll give
         permission for flight school. Come
         on. It'll be fun. You can go to
         the beach.

Dwayne looks at her. FOOTSTEPS start coming up the stairs.
Finally, he offers his hand. Sheryl shakes. Everyone is
relieved. Dwayne scribbles another note. Frank reads it.

                    FRANK
         "But...I'm...not...going...to...
         have...any...fun!!!"

He puts his hand on Dwayne's shoulder.

                    FRANK (cont'd)
         We're all with you on that one,
         Dwayne.

Olive re-enters, lugging her suitcase -- she is breathless,
flushed with excitement.

                    OLIVE
         Grandpa? Is Grandpa coming to
         California?

                    SHERYL
         We're all coming.

                    RICHARD
         Sheryl, wait. Olive, come here.
         Have a seat.

Olive walks over and sits next to Richard.

                    RICHARD (cont'd)
         Now there's no sense in entering a
         contest if you don't think you're
         gonna win. Do you think you can
         win Little Miss Sunshine?

Sheryl starts to object, but Richard raises his hand, cutting her off. Olive doesn't seem so sure.

                    RICHARD (cont'd)
          Yes or no, Olive. Are you gonna win?

Olive thinks it over. Then, with white-hot determination:

                    OLIVE
               Yes!

Richard smiles and slaps the table.

                    RICHARD
          We're goin' to California!

27   INT. LIVING ROOM - NIGHT   27

Sheryl finishes making up a bed on the fold-out sofa in the living room. Grandpa watches appreciatively.

                    SHERYL
          There, Edwin. I hope you're comfy.

                    GRANDPA
          Thank you, Sheryl. You're a fine
          woman and I'm sorry you married my
          son.

Frank enters wearing a pair of monogrammed silk pajamas.

                    FRANK
          Sheryl. Thanks. Sorry to put you
          through...

                    SHERYL
          No, Frank, you know -- we're just
          glad you're here.

They smile at each other. He gives her a kiss.

                    FRANK
               G'night.

                    SHERYL
               'Night.

28   INT. DWAYNE'S BEDROOM - NIGHT   28

Frank enters. Dwayne is on his bed reading his dog-eared copy of THUS SPOKE ZARATHUSTRA. Frank sits on the cot and takes out a padded black satin sleeping mask.

                    FRANK
          Good night, Dwayne.

Dwayne sits up and looks at Frank.

> FRANK (cont'd)
> What?

Dwayne picks up his pad and shows it to Frank. It reads:

> "Please don't kill
> yourself tonight."

Frank smiles.

> FRANK (cont'd)
> Not on your watch. I wouldn't do
> that to you.

Dwayne nods, relieved. He scribbles another note. It reads:

> "Welcome to Hell."

> FRANK (cont'd)
> (deadpan)
> Thanks, Dwayne. That means a lot
> coming from you. Good night again.

Dwayne smiles. Frank puts on his sleeping mask, lies back
and pulls the sleeping bag over him. Dwayne leans over and
turns out the light.

29   INT. VW BUS - ON THE ROAD - DAY   29

Richard is driving. Sheryl rides shotgun. Frank and Olive
sit in the second row. Dwayne and Grandpa sit in back.

Dwayne is wearing a T-shirt that says, "Jesus Was Wrong".

Olive wears a large set of headphones that completely cover
her ears. She does little half-dancing moves to the music.

No one says anything. They've been driving a while.

Grandpa's arms hang limply by his side.

> GRANDPA
> Jesus, I'm tired. I am so fucking
> tired.
> (to Dwayne)
> You know how tired I am? If some
> girl came up to me...begged me to
> fuck her...I couldn't do it.
> That's how tired I am.

> RICHARD
> Dad! Your language...! Please!

                    GRANDPA
          She's listening to music...!
                    (loud)
          Hey, Olive! I'll give you a
          million dollars if you turn around!

Olive is oblivious.

                    RICHARD
          Okay, but still, the rest of us...

                    GRANDPA
          Ahhh, the rest of you...
                    (to Dwayne)
          Can I give you some advice?
                    (Dwayne shakes his head)
          I'll do it anyway. I don't want
          you making the same mistakes I did
          when I was young.

                    RICHARD
          Great. I can't wait to hear this.

                    GRANDPA
          Dwayne? That's your name, right?
          This is the voice of experience
          talking. Are you listening?
                    (Dwayne nods)
          Kid: Fuck a lot of women. Not just
          one woman. A lot of women. You're
          young...

                    RICHARD
          Okay, Dad? I think that's enough.

                    GRANDPA
                    (ignores him)
          You gettin' any right now? Tell
          me, really. You gettin' any?

Dwayne shakes his head. Frank, amused, can't help but turn
around to watch this conversation take place.

                    GRANDPA (cont'd)
          Jesus! You're, what? Fifteen?
          You should be gettin' that young
          stuff. There's nothing in the
          world better than the young stuff!

                    RICHARD
          Okay, Dad, enough. Stop it!

                    GRANDPA
          Would you kindly not interrupt me,
          Richard?
                    (MORE)

GRANDPA (cont'd)
            (to Dwayne)
Look: right now, you're jailbait, they're
jailbait. So it's fine. The minute you
turn eighteen -- Bam! You're lookin' at
three to five.

                RICHARD
Dad, I'm gonna pull over...

                GRANDPA
So pull over! You're not gonna
shut me up! Fuck you! I lived 80
years! I'll say what I want. I
still got Nazi bullets in my ass...

                RICHARD
We know about your Nazi bullets...

                GRANDPA
You're like those fuckers at Sunset
Manor...!

                FRANK
What happened at Sunset Manor?

                SHERYL
Frank, don't encourage him.

                GRANDPA
I'll tell you what happened! I pay
my money, they let me in. I should
be able to do what the fuck I want!

                SHERYL
He started snorting heroin.

                FRANK
You started snorting heroin?!

                GRANDPA
I'm eighty!

                FRANK
You know, that stuff'll kill you.

                GRANDPA
What am I, an idiot?
            (to Dwayne)
And don't you get ideas. When you're
young, you're crazy to do that shit.

                FRANK
What about you?

                    GRANDPA
          Me?! I'm old! You get to be my
          age -- you're crazy <u>not</u> to do it.

Frank looks at Sheryl -- You're letting this happen? Sheryl
waves her hands, exasperated.

                    SHERYL
          We've tried, believe me. The
          intervention was a fiasco. He's
          worse than a two year old.

Olive sees Frank grinning at Grandpa. She takes off her
headphones and turns around.

                    OLIVE
          What are you guys talking about?

                    GRANDPA
          Politics.

                    OLIVE
          Oh.

A beat. She puts her headphones back on.

                    GRANDPA
                 (to Dwayne)
          Fuck a lot of women, kid. I got no
          reason to lie to you. Not just one
          woman. A <u>lot</u> of women.

30   INT. DINER - DAY   30

Everyone sits in a round booth, looking at menus.

                    OLIVE
          Mom, how much can we spend?

                    SHERYL
          I'd say four dollars. Anything
          under four.

Olive nods. A WAITRESS arrives.

                    WAITRESS
          Hi, you ready?

                    RICHARD
          Yeah. Number five. And coffee.

                    SHERYL
          Number seven, over easy. And
          grapefruit juice.

                    FRANK
          Fruit plate. And you have
          chamomile? With honey. Thanks.

                    GRANDPA
          The Lumberjack. Coffee. Extra
          bacon.

                    RICHARD
          Dad...

                    SHERYL
          Richard, don't start...

                    RICHARD
          He's gonna kill himself...!

                    SHERYL
          It's his life.

                    GRANDPA
          Thank you, Sheryl.

She shrugs. Dwayne holds up his note pad.

                    WAITRESS
          Garden salad? And you?

                    OLIVE
          Um... Sorry! I'm sorry!

                    WAITRESS
          Take your time...!

                    RICHARD
          Don't apologize, Olive. It's a
          sign of weakness.

Frank rolls his eyes. Olive sees something.

                    OLIVE
          Oh, oh! I want waffles. And...
          what does "A la mod-ee" mean?

                    WAITRESS
          It means it comes with ice-cream.

                    OLIVE
          Okay! A la mod-ee!

                    SHERYL
          Olive. For breakfast?

                    OLIVE
          You said, "Four dollars"!

                        SHERYL
        Okay, fine. You're right.

                        WAITRESS
        Okay! Be right back!

She departs.

                        FRANK
        Actually, Olive...? "A la mode" in French
        translates literally as "in the fashion".
        A...la...mode. Mode is derived from the
        Latin "modus", meaning due or proper
        measure. There's kind of a funny story
        about...

                        RICHARD
                (cutting in)
        Frank...? Shut up.

                        SHERYL
        Richard...!

Frank waves Sheryl off: don't bother. Richard turns to Olive.

                        RICHARD
        Olive, can I tell you something
        about ice-cream?
                (she nods)
        Ice cream is made from cream, which
        comes from cow's milk. And cream
        has a lot of fat in it...

                        SHERYL
        Richard...

                        RICHARD
        What? "She's gonna find out
        anyway." Right?

                        OLIVE
        Find out what?

                        RICHARD
        Well, when you eat ice-cream, the
        fat in the ice-cream becomes fat on
        your body...

                        SHERYL
        Richard, I swear to God...!

                        OLIVE
        What? What's wrong?

                              SHERYL
                    Nothing, honey. Nothing's wrong.

                              RICHARD
                    So if you eat lots of ice-cream,
                    you're gonna become big and fat.
                    But if you don't, you'll probably
                    stay nice and skinny.

Sheryl puts her head in her hands.

                              GRANDPA
                    Olive, Richard's an idiot. I like
                    a woman with meat on her bones.

Olive is confused.

                              OLIVE
                    I don't... Mom! Why is everyone
                    so upset?

                              SHERYL
                    I'm not upset, honey. I just want
                    you to understand: It's okay to be
                    skinny, and it's okay to be fat, if
                    that's how you want to be.
                    Whatever you want -- it's okay.

Richard rolls his eyes.

                              RICHARD
                    Okay, but, Olive, let me ask you: the
                    women in Miss America...? Are they
                    skinny, or are they fat?

                              OLIVE
                    Well... They're skinny, I guess.

                              RICHARD
                    Okay! So they probably don't eat a
                    lot of ice-cream. Do they?

Just then, the waitress arrives with a tray.

                              WAITRESS
                    Okay: Coffee, coffee, grapefruit,
                    chamomile. And here's your ice-
                    cream. A la mod-ee, right? I'll
                    have your waffles in a sec!

She departs. Olive stares at the ice-cream. Finally:

                              OLIVE
                    Does anyone want my ice-cream?

Sheryl just closes her eyes. Grandpa jumps in.

                    GRANDPA
          Yeah, I'll have a bite. You mind?
          Dwayne? Frank? Olive's giving
          away her ice-cream here.

Dwayne and Frank quickly snap to.

                    FRANK
          You mind if I have a little?

Olive shakes her head. Frank and Dwayne dig in. Even Sheryl
gets in on the act. Richard is not amused.

                    GRANDPA
              (loudly)
          Mmmm! I feel sorry for the people
          at this table who aren't enjoying
          ice-cream early in the morning.
          Olive, you're not giving away all
          your ice cream, are you? You'll
          have lonely waffles in your
          stomach! C'mon, have a bite.

                    OLIVE
          Wait. Don't take it all! Stop!

Olive picks up her spoon, fights them off. She takes a bite.

                    RICHARD
          Olive...

                    SHERYL
          Richard...!

Sheryl glares at him, ferocious. Richard shuts up.

31   EXT. PARKING LOT - DAY   31

Richard -- anxious -- listens to a greeting on his cell
phone. A small BEEP.

                    RICHARD
              (into phone)
          Stan! Richard! Look, I know you're
          busy, but we're dying to hear what
          kind of numbers you came up with in
          Scottsdale. Call me when you can.

He clicks off as Sheryl, Olive and the others exit the diner.

                    SHERYL
          You get him?

                    RICHARD
          I can't get a signal.

They trudge across the parking lot to the VW van.

                    SHERYL
          Honey, I'll drive a while.

                    RICHARD
          No, it's okay...

                    SHERYL
          No, you're right. I gotta learn to
          drive a shift. I mean, you're
          doing it. How hard can it be?

32   INT. VW BUS - PARKED - DAY   32

     Sheryl is trying to back up the bus. She's grinding gears.

                    RICHARD
          Push the stick down hard!

                    SHERYL
          I'm pushing hard!

                    RICHARD
          Put the clutch in all the way!

                    SHERYL
          It's on the floor!

                                             JUMP CUT TO:

     Richard tries. He keeps grinding gears as well. It's a
     horrible sound.

33   INT. SERVICE STATION GARAGE - DAY   33

     Richard and Sheryl talk to a Mechanic whose shirt-tag reads,
     "Stoney".

     Behind them, Olive and Grandpa are playing the game where you
     try to slap the other person's wrists. When Grandpa gets
     hit, he reacts with cries of pain -- much to Olive's delight.

     In the background, across the lot, Dwayne and Frank sit on a
     cinderblock wall, waiting for the situation to resolve itself.

                    STONEY
          Well, you got a problem. Your
          clutch is shot.

                    RICHARD
          Can we get a new one?

                              STONEY
                Well, I tell you what: These old
                buses? We'd have to order it.

                              RICHARD
                How long'd that take?

                              STONEY
                Well, it's the weekend, so...
                Maybe Thursday?

Richard and Sheryl react.

34   EXT. SERVICE STATION - DAY   34

Frank and Dwayne sit silently. Dwayne watches bitterly --
this is just one more fiasco he's been dragged into.

Frank looks on wistfully as Sheryl -- thirty yards away --
glances worriedly between Richard and the Mechanic. He
notices Dwayne's stare. He speaks without looking at Dwayne.

                              FRANK
                I don't know if you know this, but
                growing up? Your Mom was the cool
                one. She turned me on to Proust.
                She could've done anything.

Dwayne looks at Frank -- he can't quite believe this. He
takes out his pad, half-smirking, and writes:

                    "What happened?"

Frank looks at the pad, then at Dwayne.

                              FRANK (cont'd)
                She had you, Dwayne.

He pats Dwayne on the leg, gets up, and walks back towards
Richard and Sheryl. Dwayne is left alone, taking this in.

35   INT. SERVICE STATION GARAGE - DAY   35

Frank wanders in as Richard presses onward.

                              RICHARD
                Okay, look: we've come two hundred
                miles... Is there a dealership
                around here?

                              STONEY
                Well, you could call over to San
                Mateo, but they're probably closed.
                Y'know, it's the weekend.

                    RICHARD
          Yes, we're all aware of that.

Silence. The Mechanic feels bad for them. Dwayne re-enters.

                    STONEY
          Well, I tell you what: these old
          buses? You don't need a clutch to
          shift from third to fourth. You
          just ease up on the gas. You only
          really need the clutch for first
          and second.

Richard doesn't understand what he's getting at.

                    STONEY (cont'd)
          What I'm sayin' is: as long as you
          keep parkin' on a hill, you get
          yourself goin' fifteen, twenty
          miles an hour, and you just start
          up in third. Then you shift
          between third and fourth.

                    RICHARD
          And you can drive like that?

                    STONEY
          Oh, yeah. The problem's just
          getting up that speed up. As long
          as you keep parkin' it on a hill,
          you're fine. My brother and I once
          drove from here to Canada...

                    RICHARD
          What if you're not on a hill?

                    STONEY
          What?

                    RICHARD
          I mean, it's sitting here right now.
          There's no hill. How do we...?

The Mechanic -- Stoney -- considers this. He squints his
eyes and runs his tongue back and forth across his teeth.

                    STONEY
          Well, I tell you what: You get
          enough people -- you just get
          behind there and push. Just push
          it up to ten, fifteen miles an
          hour, and you just go. Everybody
          jump inside, and you just go!

They all stare at him.

36   EXT. PARKING LOT - DAY   36

Richard's at the wheel of the bus. Everyone else, including
Stoney, is behind the bus. The sliding door is open.

                    RICHARD
          Okay, ready?! Olive, Dad: I want
          you in the car first.

                    OLIVE
          I know. We know.

                    RICHARD
          Okay, is everyone ready?

                    SHERYL
          Yes! Let's go!

Richard starts up the bus. Frank turns to the others.

                    FRANK
          I just want everyone here to know
          I'm the pre-eminent Proust scholar
          in the United States.

                    RICHARD
          Okay, go! Push!

They all push. The van starts rolling, slow at first, then
faster and faster. Finally, they're all running behind it.

                    RICHARD (cont'd)
          Olive, Dad, get in! Sheryl!

Olive, Grandpa, and Sheryl jump in the side door. The
Mechanic fades. Frank and Dwayne keep pushing faster.

                    RICHARD (cont'd)
          Okay, I'm puttin' it into gear!

He guns the engine and shifts from neutral to third. The bus
is REVVING low but is powering itself nonetheless.

                    SHERYL
          Okay, get in! Get in!
                (to Richard)
          Slow down! You're losing them!

                    RICHARD
          I can't! I can't slow down!

Dwayne runs up to the door. He sees Frank is fading.

He runs back to Frank, gets behind him, and pushes him up
alongside the bus. Frank dives in. Dwayne dives after him.

37   INT. VW BUS - ON THE ROAD - DAY   37

    Everyone cheers. Frank is panting. Dwayne shuts the door.

> RICHARD
> Is that it? Are we in?

> FRANK
> (to Dwayne)
> "No one gets left behind! No one
> gets left behind!" Outstanding,
> soldier! Outstanding!

    Frank salutes him. Dwayne smiles, embarrassed.

38   INT./EXT. VW BUS, ON THE ROAD - DAY - DRIVING MONTAGE   38

    The VW drives down an on-ramp onto the Interstate.

    The VW cruises down I-40. Signs pass. Scenery goes by.

    Inside the bus, everyone just stares out the windows.

    Later, Grandpa is doing magic tricks for Olive. He produces
a quarter from behind her ear and gives it to her.

    Later, everyone is playing rock, paper, scissors.

    Still later, everyone is back to doing nothing.

39   INT. VW BUS - ON THE ROAD - DAY   39

    Richard is pitching his business to Frank, who is bored, but
not as bored as he would be doing nothing. He is slouched
down, barely moving. Richard, however, is in full sell mode.

> RICHARD
> ...So I start pitching The Nine Steps to
> Stan Grossman... Two minutes in, he stops
> me, says, "I can sell this."

> FRANK
> Wow...!

> RICHARD
> This is the guy who knows how to do it --
> start with the book; then media tour,
> corporate events, videos... There's a
> science in how you roll these things out.

> FRANK
> Interesting...!

                         RICHARD
              He's at the Expo in Scottsdale
              right now -- building the buzz.
              He's doing a ticking clock auction.

                         FRANK
              How about that...!

                         RICHARD
              And I can detect that note of
              sarcasm, Frank...

                         FRANK
              What sarcasm?!

                         RICHARD
              ...But I just want you to know -- I
              feel sorry for you.

                         FRANK
              You do? Good.

                         RICHARD
              Because sarcasm is the refuge of
              losers.

                         FRANK
              It is?! Really?!

                         RICHARD
              Sarcasm is just the sour grapes of losers
              trying to pull winners down to their
              level. Step Four.

                         FRANK
              Wow, Richard! You've really opened my
              eyes to what a loser I am! Say, how much
              do I owe you for those pearls of wisdom?

                         RICHARD
              It's on me, buddy. It's on me.

                         SHERYL
              Okay, you guys, enough. Frank,
              stop it.

                         FRANK
                    (pointing)
              "He started it!"

     Even Sheryl has to laugh a little at this. Pretty soon,
     everyone in the back is giggling. Even Dwayne smiles.

                         SHERYL
              You are bad! You are so bad!

                    FRANK
          I know!

                    RICHARD
          Yeah, go on and laugh. You're whistling
          past the graveyard.

Richard maintains a steely composure. Then Richard's cell
phone goes off: BEEEEP-BEEEEP. He checks the number.

                    RICHARD (cont'd)
          There! That's the call!
          Everybody, please! Everyone...?!
                    (clicks the phone)
          Stan! Hello...? Hello?! <u>Hello</u>?!

40   EXT. CONVENIENCE STORE / PHONE BOOTH - DAY   40

Richard is in a phone booth at a gas station / mini-mart.
Everyone hangs out by the bus -- parked on a slight incline --
except Dwayne, who is doing push-ups on the grass nearby.

Richard waits tensely. Then -- abruptly -- he is "up".

                    RICHARD
          Stan! Richard! Yeah, yeah, no problem!
          So... What'd we get?

He listens. Gradually, his face falls.

BY THE VW -- Sheryl, Olive, Grandpa, and Frank watch Richard
on the phone. Dwayne wanders back to the van.

                    SHERYL
          Honey, I'm gonna use the ladies
          room. You need to go?

                    OLIVE
          No. I'm gonna practice my routine
          over here.

                    SHERYL
          Okay. Don't go too far.

They both wander off. Frank turns to Dwayne and Grandpa.

                    FRANK
          I'm gonna get a drink. You guys
          want anything?

Dwayne shakes his head, but Grandpa pulls out his wallet.

                    GRANDPA
          Yeah. Get me some porn. Something
          really nasty.
                    (MORE)

                              GRANDPA (cont'd)
                    None of that air-brushed shit,
                    alright? Here, here's a twenty.
                    Get a little treat for yourself
                    too, if they got any fag-rags in
                    there.

Frank stares at Grandpa. Then, stoic, he takes the twenty
and heads off. Dwayne and Grandpa turn back towards Richard.

41   INT. CONVENIENCE STORE - DAY   41

Frank stands at the counter, pointing out behind-the-counter
magazines to a middle-aged PROPRIETOR.

                              FRANK
                    That one. That one. And let's try
                    that one. No, down... Yeah, <u>that</u>
                    one. And a small grape Slushee.

By the front window, an extremely good-looking young man,
JOSH, is perusing the newsstand, cradling a grocery bag. He
stops and stares.

                              JOSH
                    Frank...?

Frank turns. They are startled to see each other. Frank
puts his arms behind his back, hiding his bandages.

                              JOSH (cont'd)
                    Oh my God! How are you? I thought you
                    were gonna be in Santa Fe for the
                    conference. I was looking for you...!

                              FRANK
                    Yeah, the conference... Something
                    came up last minute and... Those
                    things are so tedious anyway.

                              JOSH
                    Tell me about it. Wow, this is so
                    crazy! So we miss you in Santa Fe
                    and then -- bingo -- here you are!

                              FRANK
                    I know, it's just... Aren't you
                    supposed to be in New Haven?

                              JOSH
                    Yeah, well -- you heard about Larry
                    and the whole genius thing, right?
                              (jocular "air quotes")
                    "It's official." So after we got
                    the news he decided to blow a wad on
                    a getaway-type thing.
                              (MORE)

                         JOSH (cont'd)
            We're going to this private spa in
            Sedona and then...

                         FRANK
            Larry's here...?!

                         JOSH
            He's out filling the tank. He's...
            Wow, I can't believe this! How've
            you been?

                         FRANK
            Fine. I'm fine.

                         JOSH
            Good. Good. You know, I heard...
            Someone in Santa Fe told me you got
            fired...?

                         FRANK
            Yeah. No, I quit. I quit.
            Enough's enough, you know?

                         JOSH
            Right. Well, good. Good for you.
            'Cause you always seemed so...
            tense, y'know?

                         FRANK
            Yah.

                         JOSH
            So what're you up to now?

                         FRANK
            I'm... Weighing my options. You
            know. Taking time off.

                         JOSH
            Well, great. That's great.

The Proprietor puts three porn magazines and a grape Slushee
on the counter and rings them up for Frank.

                         PROPRIETOR
            $15.94, please, sir.

Josh glances at the magazines, then at Frank. Frank keeps
his hands behind his back. An excruciating pause.

                         JOSH
            Well, great seeing you again.

                         FRANK
            Yeah. You too.

                         JOSH
              Take care of yourself.

                         FRANK
              You too.

Josh turns and exits.   Frank hands over a $20 bill.

He watches Josh walk off while the Proprietor puts the
magazines in a brown wrapper and hands Frank his change.

Frank takes a few steps and peers out the window.

HIS POV -- Josh gets into a Jaguar convertible driven by a
distinguished-looking BEARDED MAN.

Josh says something and points back at the store. The
Bearded Man turns and cranes his neck.

Frank, in the store, ducks out of view. Josh and the Bearded
Man exchange a few words, then shrug and laugh.

Then they drive off. Frank watches, heartbroken. Behind
him, the Proprietor picks up the Slushee and waves it.

                         PROPRIETOR
              Ay! Don't forget your Slushee!

42   EXT. PHONE BOOTH - DAY   42

Richard is grasping at straws.

                         RICHARD
              Okay, Stan, wait... No, listen --
              are you still in Scottsdale?
              'Cause I'm coming right by you.
              Maybe I can swing by... No, Stan,
              listen...!

43   EXT. VW BUS - PARKED - DAY   43

Grandpa, standing by the bus, reads Richard's body language.
Richard, in the booth, talks with increasing desperation.

                         GRANDPA
              He's not getting it. Christ.

He and Dwayne share a look. Grandpa turns away, troubled. Frank
walks stiffly back to the bus with his Slushee and the wrapper.
Without looking, he hands the wrapper to Grandpa.

                         FRANK
              How's it going?

                         GRANDPA
              Not so good.

Sheryl walks back to the VW as Richard hangs up the phone. Richard
stays in the booth for a second. Then he exits and walks back to
the VW, passing Sheryl.

                         SHERYL
              So what happened?

                         RICHARD
              Nothing. Let's get out of here.

He walks to the driver's seat.

                         SHERYL
              Wait a minute. I thought you said
              this was a done deal.

                         RICHARD
              He said it was a done deal.

                         SHERYL
              You didn't get anything?
                   (beat)
              So where does that leave us?

                         RICHARD
              It leaves us fucked. That's where
              it leaves us.

Pause.

                         SHERYL
              I can't believe I'm hearing this.
              Did you try negotiating...?

                         RICHARD
              Yes, I tried! I tried everything!
              What do you think...?! Let's just
              go, okay? Let's get out of here!

He starts the car. She stares at him. He won't look at her.
Finally, he turns and yells:

                         RICHARD (cont'd)
              Let's go!!!

Furious, she goes and gets in the bus, slamming the door.

Everyone else gets in. Richard releases the brake and they
drift down the hill.

As the van rolls away, Richard shifts and GUNS the engine.

44   INT. VW BUS - ON THE ROAD - DAY   44

Silence. Everyone avoids everyone else's eyes. Finally,
Frank glances around.

                    FRANK
          Where's Olive?

45   EXT. PHONE BOOTH - DAY   45

Olive stands next to the phone booth.

In the distance, the VW bus appears.

It drives up and swings around the road.

Dwayne slides open the door. They barely slow down.

Olive dives in. The van coasts downhill.

Then Richard shifts into gear and GUNS the engine.

46   INT. VW BUS - ON THE ROAD - DAY   46

Richard drives. Everyone is tense except Olive, who listens
to her headphones. Finally, Grandpa gets up and walks up to
the front of the bus. He speaks quietly to Richard.

                    GRANDPA
          Richard...

                    RICHARD
          Yeah...

                    GRANDPA
          Listen, whatever happens -- at
          least you tried to do something on
          your own, which is more than most
          people ever do, and I include
          myself in that category. It takes
          guts, and I'm proud of you for
          taking the chance, okay?

                    RICHARD
          Okay, Dad. Thanks.

He tries to be cool and dismissive, but Grandpa just stands
there. Finally, Richard turns and makes eye contact.

Awkwardly, he offers his hand to Grandpa. They shake.

                    RICHARD (cont'd)
          Thanks, Dad.

47   OMIT   47

48   EXT. MOTEL - NIGHT   48

With keys in hand, they walk along the motor court, lugging
their luggage, looking for their rooms. A heavy silence.

                    SHERYL
          Here's eleven. Frank, you're
          twelve? And Grandpa's thirteen.

                    OLIVE
          Mom? Can I sleep with Grandpa?

                    SHERYL
          That's up to him.

                    OLIVE
          Grandpa...?

                    GRANDPA
          Okay. I got two beds. You could
          still use some rehearsing...

                    OLIVE
          I know! That's why I said...!

                    RICHARD
          Everyone, we're getting up at
          seven. I'll knock on your door.
          We want to be on the road by eight
          so we can be in Redondo Beach in
          time for registration. It's three
          hundred miles, so we can't dawdle.

                    SHERYL
          Frank? You guys'll be all right?

                    FRANK
          We'll be fine.

Dwayne nods. Sheryl kisses Dwayne and Olive.

                    SHERYL
          Okay. Good night. Sleep tight.

Everyone waves good night to each other.

49   INT. MOTEL ROOM ELEVEN - NIGHT   49

Sheryl and Richard enter. Sheryl closes the door.

                    RICHARD
          What a fucking nightmare...!

                    SHERYL
          Richard... We have to talk.

                    RICHARD
          Please, not now. Let's just get
          through this and get home...

                    SHERYL
          No, Richard. We need to talk now.

50   INT. MOTEL ROOM TWELVE - NIGHT   50

     Dwayne lies on his bed staring at the ceiling. Through the
     walls we can HEAR Sheryl and Richard arguing very loudly.

                    SHERYL (O.S.)
          You said it was a done deal!!!

                    RICHARD (O.S.)
          Stan Grossman gave me his word!

                    SHERYL (O.S.)
          I'm not married to Stan Grossman! Jesus,
          Richard, what're we gonna do?

                    RICHARD (O.S.)
          We just have to keep going...

                    SHERYL (O.S.)
          I can't keep going, Richard! It's too
          much! We can't keep going like this!

     Et cetera. Frank wanders out of the bathroom, squirting
     Rogaine on his head and rubbing his scalp. He watches Dwayne.

                    FRANK
          Hey. Don't listen to that. Come
          on, let's watch the tube.

     He turns on the TV. Dwayne sits up and turns the TV off. He
     lies down, stares at the ceiling again. Frank looks at him.

                    FRANK (cont'd)
          I'm gonna brush my teeth.

     He goes back to the bathroom and -- half-framed in the
     doorway, out of Dwayne's sight -- pauses before the mirror.
     Quietly, he takes out his wallet, opens it and stares at
     something.

     OVER FRANK'S SHOULDER -- He holds a photo that shows Frank
     and the young man from the convenience store, Josh, at some
     chic party, wearing tuxes, smiling, and drinking Champagne.

     Frank stands in the bathroom, shoulders slumped, not moving,
     staring at the picture. Dwayne remains on the bed, listening.

                    RICHARD (O.S.)
          I trusted him, okay?! You have to
          trust to be trusted! Step Six!

                    SHERYL (O.S.)
          Fuck the Nine Steps, Richard!
          They're not working! It's over!!!
          Forget it!!! I never want to hear
          the Nine Steps again!!!

A stunned silence. Dwayne, hearing this, just barely smiles.

51   OMIT   51

52   OMIT   52

53   INT. MOTEL ROOM THIRTEEN - NIGHT   53

Grandpa tucks Olive -- in pajamas -- into bed. It's quiet -- we
can't hear Sheryl and Richard fighting.

                    GRANDPA
          There you go. Snug as a bug in a rug.

                    OLIVE
          Grandpa...?

                    GRANDPA
          Yeah?

She hesitates.

                    OLIVE
          I'm kind of scared about tomorrow.

                    GRANDPA
          Olive, you're gonna blow 'em out of
          the water. I guarantee it. They
          won't know what hit 'em.

She smiles. He's about to leave her when...

                    OLIVE
          Grandpa...?

He turns back. She hesitates again. Finally:

                    OLIVE (cont'd)
          Am I pretty?

                    GRANDPA
          Olive... You're the most beautiful
          girl in the whole world.

> OLIVE
> No! You're just saying that!

> GRANDPA
> I'm saying it 'cause it's true!

> OLIVE
> Grandpa...!

> GRANDPA
> I can't help it! When you love
> someone, you always think they're
> beautiful!

> OLIVE
> No, you know... Tell me the truth!

> GRANDPA
> Okay, okay... You're old enough --
> I think you can handle it. I'm
> gonna tell you the truth.

He takes a deep breath. She gets very quiet. Gently:

> GRANDPA (cont'd)
> Olive... I think you're the most
> beautiful girl in the whole world!

She squeals with laughter.

> OLIVE
> No!!! Grandpa!!!

She smiles up at him. He musses her hair, starts to get up...

> OLIVE (cont'd)
> Grandpa...?

> GRANDPA
> Uh-huh?

...He sits back down. Olive opens her mouth, hesitates.
Then suddenly -- unexpectedly -- she is upset, though she
tries to hide it, turning away and fighting back tears.

Finally, she turns back and says in a tiny voice:

> OLIVE
> I don't want to be a loser.

> GRANDPA
> You're not a loser, Olive! Why do
> you say that?!

OLIVE
Because...! Dad hates losers.
That's what he said!

GRANDPA
But you're not a loser! And your
Dad would never hate you, ever!

OLIVE
But what if I lose tomorrow?

She's on the verge of tears.

GRANDPA
Whoa, whoa, back up a sec. You can't lose.
You know why? A real loser isn't someone
who doesn't win. A real loser is someone
so afraid of not winning they don't even
try. That's not you! You're gonna dance,
right?! So even if you win, or you don't
win, you've already won! See? You see?
You-see-you-see-you-see?

He tickles her. She squeals. He stops. She recovers. He
brushes her hair back.

GRANDPA (cont'd)
A real loser doesn't try. And
you're trying, right?
(she nods)
So you're not a loser, are you?

She shakes her head. They smile at each other.

GRANDPA (cont'd)
I think we're gonna have fun
tomorrow.
(she nods)
I'm gonna get ready for bed. Good
night. Sleep tight.

OLIVE
Don't let the bedbugs bite!

He gives her a kiss, turns off the lamp.

54   INT. MOTEL BATHROOM - DAY   54

Grandpa enters and locks the door. He opens his shaving kit
and takes out a small mirror and a tiny ziploc baggie filled
with light brown powder.

55   INT. MOTEL ROOM ELEVEN - NIGHT   55

Richard and Sheryl sit on opposite sides of the bed. It's
quiet. They've hit rock bottom. A moment of silence.

Sheryl stares at the floor -- troubled and deeply unhappy.

> SHERYL
> Maybe we should try living apart.
> Just for a while.

Richard closes his eyes. This kills him. Abruptly, he
stands, gathers his keys, wallet, etc.

> SHERYL (cont'd)
> What're you doing? Richard...?

> RICHARD
> I'm gonna fix this.

> SHERYL
> Richard...

> RICHARD
> Don't worry. I'm gonna fix this.

He grabs his coat and exits, very determined. Sheryl, left
behind, flops back on the bed.

56   EXT. MOTEL PARKING LOT - NIGHT   56

Richard strides to the VW bus, parked parallel on the street.

A small crowd of TEENAGERS is hanging out, smoking and
drinking. Three Teen Boys are puttering around on mopeds.

Richard -- on a mission -- climbs in the VW's driver's seat
and starts it up. He shifts into third and REVS the engine.
The VW doesn't move. He REVS it very high and loud, jostling
in his seat to try to get the bus going. It stays still.

Richard takes his foot off the gas, slumps back.

The Teens stop chatting and stare at him. Richard, at the end
of his rope, turns and looks at the Teens and their mopeds.

> JUMP TO:

Richard walks up to the Teens on their mopeds. They are
wary. Richard smiles, tries to be friendly.

> RICHARD
> Hey! How would one of you guys
> like to make twenty dollars?

The Teens look at each other.

                    TEEN BOY
          Fuck off, fag.

This amuses the other Teens. Richard -- undeterred -- pulls
out his wallet, opens it up.

                    RICHARD
          Okay, look...

                                                    CUT TO:

57   EXT. HIGHWAY ENTRANCE - NIGHT - LONG SHOT   57

An empty highway entrance, lit by street lamps. Interstate
traffic flies by at 70 mph -- cars, SUVs, eighteen wheelers.

Into the frame and down the entrance ramp rides Richard,
balanced precariously on a borrowed moped, pushing 35 mph.

He edges into the break-down lane and drives parallel to the
SWOOSHING traffic, a look of grim determination on his face.

He passes a sign that reads, "Scottsdale, 23 Miles."

                                            FADE TO BLACK

58   EXT. MOTEL BALCONY - NIGHT   58

It's quiet. A bare motel balcony, lit by a single street
lamp. Sheryl, smoking a cigarette, stares up at the stars.

She looks at her wedding ring, jiggles it with her thumb.

FADE IN the WHINE of a moped.

59   EXT. HOTEL PARKING LOT - NIGHT   59

Richard pulls into the parking lot of a large chain hotel. A
marquee out front reads, "Power / Life Expo. Welcome!"

60   INT. HOTEL HALLWAY - NIGHT   60

Richard comes in a side exit and strides down a long,
carpeted hallway. Empty conference rooms line the hall.

Outside each conference room is an easel with a foam board
mock-up of a self-help book cover. Richard walks past face
after face of aspiring self-help gurus.

61   INT. HOTEL LOBBY - NIGHT   61

Richard -- windblown, still in shorts and sneakers -- strides
into a well-appointed lobby. A female CONCIERGE is on late-
night duty. He walks to a courtesy phone, picks it up.

                    RICHARD
                 (into phone)
         Stan Grossman, please. Thank you.

Through the receiver, we hear RINGING. Then VOICE-MAIL.

                    VOICE MAIL
                 (via phone)
         The hotel guest you're calling is
         not available. Please leave a
         message at the tone.

BEEP.

                    RICHARD
         Stan, it's Richard...
                 (at a loss)
         I don't know where the fuck you
         are. I'm at your hotel. Call me.

He hangs up and looks around, exasperated. He takes out his
cell phone and dials. He puts the phone to his ear.

As the phone RINGS in his ear, we hear the synchronized
BLEATING of a cell phone from the hotel bar nearby.

It takes Richard a second to make the connection. He turns.

62   INT HOTEL BAR - NIGHT   62

In the bar/lounge, a boisterous group of CORPORATE TYPES --
prosperously attired men, meticulously groomed women -- are
seated around a booth, drinking and laughing together.

Holding court is Stan Grossman, a swarthy mid-30s go-getter
wearing khakis, loafers, and a cashmere V-neck.

Richard watches as Stan pulls out his cell phone, checks the
caller ID, shakes his head, puts the phone away.

Richard -- phone in his ear -- walks over and stands behind
Stan Grossman, staring down at him. The Corporate Types stop
laughing. Stan turns, looks up at Richard. Richard smiles.

                    RICHARD
         Hi, Stan!

63   EXT. HOTEL POOL - NIGHT   63

          Richard and Stan stand on the edge of the pool apron,
          arguing.

                              RICHARD
                    You said it would <u>sell</u>...!

                              STAN GROSSMAN
                    That's what I <u>thought</u>! At the <u>time</u>!

                              RICHARD
                    But it's a great program! You said
                    yourself! I don't understand...!

                              STAN GROSSMAN
                    It's not the program, Richard.
                    It's you, okay? No one's heard of
                    you. Nobody cares.

          Richard exhales, shakes his head, gathers himself.

                              RICHARD
                    So what's the next step?

                              STAN GROSSMAN
                    There is none. We had our shot.
                    It didn't fly. We move on.

                              RICHARD
                    You mean give up.

                              STAN GROSSMAN
                    Richard...

                              RICHARD
                    One set back, you're ready to quit.

                              STAN GROSSMAN
                    Richard, listen -- I pushed this
                    thing hard, okay? I rammed it down
                    their fucking throats, all right?
                    No one bought it. Now, I know the
                    market. It's time to move on.
                    You're not gonna win this one.

          Richard stares at Stan, absorbing this. Then he speaks with
          a strained nonchalance, nodding and smiling.

                              RICHARD
                    Okay...! Good! I'm glad. You
                    know why? <u>This</u> is what the Nine
                    Steps are all about...

STAN GROSSMAN
                Richard! Jesus...!

                       RICHARD
                You blew it, Stan. You're out.

Richard turns and walks off. Stan can't believe it. He
shakes his head and re-enters the hotel.

64   EXT. HIGHWAY - NIGHT   64

      Richard, grim, rides his borrowed moped along the breakdown
      lane as cars and trucks ROAR past him.

      This is -- hands down -- the worst moment of his life.

      There's a FLASH of lightning and a CLAP of thunder. It
      starts to rain. Richard keeps riding.

65   INT. MOTEL - NIGHT   65

      A darkened motel room. We hear the WHINE of the moped as it
      pulls into the parking lot and up to the door.

      The door opens and Richard -- dazed, soaking wet -- steps in.

      He closes the door behind him, walks over, lies on the bed --
      fully clothed -- and stares up at the ceiling.

      Sheryl, sleeping, wakes up and sees Richard.

                       SHERYL
                Y'okay?

      He nods. Sheryl rubs his arm, rolls over, goes back to
      sleep. Richard stares up at the ceiling.

                                              FADE TO BLACK

                       OLIVE (V.O.)
                Dad...?

66   INT. MOTEL ROOM - DAWN   66

      Richard opens his eyes. Olive is standing next to the bed.
      The blue light of dawn is coming through the windows.

                       RICHARD
                What is it, hon...?

                       OLIVE
                Grandpa won't wake up.

      Richard takes this in.

67   EXT. AMBULANCE ROOF - DAY   67

      We are behind the lights of an ambulance as it speeds down a
      commercial strip. The LIGHTS FLASH and SIREN BLARES.

68   INT. HOSPITAL WAITING ROOM - DAY   68

      Everyone sits silently in a waiting room, waiting for news.

      Olive, bored, goes through a rack of medical flyers. She
      takes one and approaches Dwayne.

                          OLIVE
                You want to take an eye test?
                          (Dwayne shakes his head)
                Uncle Frank? You want to take an
                eye test?

                          SHERYL
                Olive, come here. Put that away.
                We're gonna have a family meeting.
                Dwayne? Family meeting.

                          RICHARD
                What? Now?

                          SHERYL
                Richard... Let's just do it.

      She takes a breath. She turns to the kids.

                          SHERYL (cont'd)
                First of all, the doctors are doing
                everything they can to help Grandpa right
                now. He's had a long...
                          (searches for words)
                ...eventful life, and I know he
                loves both of you very much. But
                if God wants to take him, we have
                to be ready to accept that, okay?
                          (they nod)
                Now, I think you guys know we've been
                having money problems lately, with
                Richard's venture and everything...
                Things haven't really gone the way we
                hoped. So it looks like when we get home
                we might have to make some changes in the
                way we live. We might have to move out of
                our house. We might have to declare
                bankruptcy. I don't know. I have to talk
                to a lawyer about all that.

      She looks at Richard, the kids. Her voice becomes shaky.

SHERYL (cont'd)
But whatever happens -- we're a
family. What's important is that
we love each other. I love you
guys so, so, so much...

She turns away, starts to cry. Frank puts his hand on her
shoulder. Sheryl grasps it. Olive and Dwayne watch Sheryl.

Dwayne writes a note, shows it to Olive. It reads:

"Go hug Mom!"

Olive goes and hugs Sheryl. Sheryl, crying, picks up Olive
and holds her in her lap, hugging her. Dwayne gets up, goes
across the waiting room and stares out the window.

OUT THE WINDOW

It's a banal suburban landscape. Cars go busily back and
forth on a distant road.

Dwayne just stares out the window with a blank face. Behind
him, a DOCTOR enters the waiting area.

DOCTOR
Are you the family of Edwin Hoover?

69   INT. HOSPITAL WAITING ROOM - MOMENTS LATER   69

The Doctor takes a breath.

DOCTOR
I'm sorry. We did everything we
could. He was... It was too much.
He probably fell asleep and never
woke up. I'll have someone come
talk about handling the remains.

RICHARD
Thank you. Appreciate it.

The Doctor opens the door and calls down the hall.

DOCTOR
Linda...!

He gestures, then departs. Silence.

OLIVE
Is Grandpa dead?

SHERYL
Yeah, honey. He's passed away.

Olive nods, says nothing.

A hospital administrator, LINDA, comes in with a sheaf of papers. She is overburdened and all business.

                    LINDA
          Hi, I'm your bereavement liaison, Linda.
          My consolations for your loss.

                    RICHARD
          Thank you, Linda.

Linda hands Richard her sheaf of paperwork.

                    LINDA
                 (fast)
          Okay. These are the forms you need
          to fill out -- death certificate,
          report of death and the M.E. pink
          slip. Try and be as detailed as
          possible. This is a brochure for
          our Grief Recovery Support Group
          that meets Tuesdays. If you'd
          like, I can refer you at this time
          to a funeral home so you can begin
          making arrangements.

Richard and Sheryl glance at each other.

                    RICHARD
          Actually, pre-arrangements have
          been made in Albuquerque.

                    LINDA
          Albuquerque...?

                    RICHARD
          Yeah, we're passing through. Y'see, we're
          trying to get to California...

                    LINDA
          Okay -- if the body is crossing
          state lines? You're gonna need a
          Burial Transit Permit from the
          County Registrar...

                    RICHARD
          Okay, fine, but here's the thing --
          we're trying to get to Redondo
          Beach by three this afternoon...

                    LINDA
          Three o'clock? Today?
                 (checks her watch)
          That ain't gonna happen.

                              RICHARD
                    But... This is for my daughter.
                    It's really important.

                              LINDA
                    It may be important, but you still
                    have to fill out this paperwork.

                              RICHARD
                    Okay, look, I know this is unusual...
                    Is there a way we can go and come back?
                    I mean, can we do paperwork later?

                              LINDA
                    You can't abandon the body...

          RICHARD   LINDA
I'm not gonna abandon the   ...Otherwise the hospital
body. I just want to go and   becomes responsible... Sir,
come back. We just need to   there's a way these things
go and then we'll come back!   need to be done. Sir?
We'll come back!   Sir...? Sir!!!

                              LINDA (cont'd)
                    You're not the only one who's had someone
                    die here today, all right?! Now we have a
                    way of doing things around here, and I'm
                    gonna ask you to respect our procedures!

Silence. Richard stares at the floor, seething. Pause.

                              RICHARD
                    Could you...? Is there a way we could
                    view the remains?

                              LINDA
                         (nods, also restrained)
                    I'll show you, yes.

She leads them out.

70   INT. HOSPITAL CORRIDOR - DAY   70

Linda stops in front of an intensive care room.

                              LINDA
                    He's in here. We haven't had a
                    chance to move him downstairs yet.
                    Now someone may come by in a few
                    minutes to take him to the
                    basement, but just tell them who
                    you are. They'll wait.

                              RICHARD
                    Thank you.

> LINDA
> When you're done with the paperwork
> I'll be in the nurse's station.

> RICHARD
> Okay. Great. Thank you, Linda.

She departs.

71   INT. INTENSIVE CARE ROOM - DAY   71

They enter. It's quiet. There's a body under a sheet.

Richard walks over and peers under it, puts it down.

He turns away and faces the wall. He starts hyperventilating
-- choking down the emotion. He doesn't want to lose
control, and he's not comfortable showing his feelings.

> RICHARD
> (under his breath)
> Goddamn it, Dad. Goddamn it.
> (beat)
> Stupid, stupid, stupid...!!!

He shakes his head and takes a few sharp breaths, getting
himself under control -- still facing the wall.

Sheryl hugs Olive, stroking her hair. Olive is dry-eyed --
this is all new to her. Sheryl bends down and whispers:

> SHERYL
> We'll do Little Miss Sunshine next
> year. Okay, honey? Next year.

Olive nods. No one says anything. Finally, Richard turns
around. He is very determined.

> RICHARD
> No. We've come seven hundred miles. I'll
> be damned if I'm not making that contest.

> SHERYL
> Honey... We can't leave him!

> RICHARD
> We're not going to leave him.

Richard dumps the paperwork in a wastebasket. He opens the
door, glances into the hallway. He closes the door.

> RICHARD (cont'd)
> Fuck...!

He looks desperately around the room. He sees the window.

He goes to the window, opens it up.

72   EXT. HOSPITAL - DAY   72

Richard peers out the window. He's at the back side of the
building, seven or eight feet above a near-empty parking lot.

73   INT. INTENSIVE CARE ROOM - DAY   73

Richard ducks back in. He tosses his car keys to Dwayne.

                    RICHARD
          Dwayne. Go around outside.

                    SHERYL
          Richard... What are you thinking?

                    RICHARD
          We'll take him with us.

                    SHERYL
          No, Richard. No. That's not going
          to happen.

                    RICHARD
          He's better off with us than with these
          people!
                    (to Dwayne)
          Go under the window. Frank, you go with
          him.

                    SHERYL
          Dwayne, don't you dare!
                    (to Richard)
          Look: you stay here. We'll take
          Olive. Frank'll drive!

                    RICHARD
          Whose gonna push the bus to get it
          started, huh? One stoplight and
          you're screwed.
                    (never say die:)
          Listen to me, everyone. If there's
          one thing Grandpa would've wanted,
          it's to have Olive perform at the
          Little Miss Sunshine pageant. I
          believe we'd be doing a grave
          disservice to his memory if we gave
          up now. There's two kinds of people
          in the world: winners and losers.
          And what's the difference? Winners
          don't give up. So what are we here?
          Are we winners? Or losers?

                                            CUT TO:

EXT. HOSPITAL - DAY

Richard leans out the window.

> RICHARD
> Okay, ready?

Frank, Dwayne, Sheryl and Olive stand under the window, trying to look inconspicuous. Frank gestures -- Wait.

Across the lot, two NURSES stroll toward the hospital.

> FRANK
> Not yet... Not yet...

The Nurses pass out of sight.

> FRANK (cont'd)
> Okay -- go, go, go!

Richard disappears for a second, then reappears with a big bundle wrapped in a sheet. He hoists it into the window.

> RICHARD
> Careful... Careful...

He edges the bundle off the window ledge. Frank and Dwayne gently lower the bundle to the ground. They glance around.

> FRANK
> Okay! Here we go! One, two...

Frank, Dwayne, Sheryl and Olive lift the bundle together and scuttle across the parking lot to the VW bus fifty feet away.

An ELDERLY COUPLE walking fifty yards away observes them.

> FRANK (cont'd)
> Be cool. Be cool. Almost there.

They arrive at the bus.

Dwayne whips open the VW's back door (a hatchback that hides your luggage) and they hoist the bundle in. Frank slams the door closed. Richard comes sprinting into the parking lot.

> RICHARD
> Okay, let's roll! You ready?

> FRANK
> Any time, Rich!

Richard starts up the bus, gets out and helps them push.

They get the bus rolling. The lot is at a slight incline,
which helps. Finally, Richard jumps behind the wheel.

                    RICHARD
          Okay, I'm putting it into gear...!

Sheryl and Olive jump in the side door. Frank and Dwayne run
behind the bus, pushing like crazy.

                    FRANK
          Did I mention I'm the pre-eminent
          Proust scholar in the US?

Richard REVS the engine and puts it in third. The bus begins
picking up speed. Dwayne and Frank sprint along side.

This time, Dwayne is prepared to push Frank up along-side the
bus. Frank lunges in. Dwayne jumps in after him.

75   INT. VW BUS - DAY   75

Dwayne slides the door shut. They're all giddy and
breathless from the escape.

They gradually sober up. Olive is thinking.

                    OLIVE
          Dad? What's gonna happen to Grandpa?

                    RICHARD
          Honey, as soon as we get to Redondo
          I'm gonna call a funeral home in
          Albuquerque and they'll take care of
          everything. Your Grandpa was smart
          and planned ahead. Okay?

Olive nods. That's not really what she was asking about.
Sheryl sees this.

                    SHERYL
          Honey, Grandpa's soul is in Heaven
          now. He's with God. Okay?

Olive nods. She turns and looks out the window.

OUT THE WINDOW

The passing landscape of the road leading back to the
Interstate. It seems a long way from God.

CLOSE ON OLIVE

Thinking.

Begin MUSIC -- the same quiet tune that began the film.

76   OMIT   76

77   OMIT (MERGED WITH 75)   77

The dialogue below plays over the following shots.

The family drives in silence, each looking out the window.

Richard drives -- stoic, determined.

Sheryl is pensive. She sneaks glances at Richard.

Frank, subdued, watches Sheryl. He rubs Olive on the head.

Olive, headphones around her neck, stares out the window.

Dwayne lies across the back seat, staring up.

DWAYNE'S POV -- Passing power lines undulate against the sky.

From the back, we see the highway passing as each person is
lost in a reverie.

Sheryl, in the front, looks at Richard, reaches over and rubs
Richard's neck. Richard glances at her, keeps driving.

> OLIVE (V.O.)
> Uncle Frank?

> FRANK (V.O.)
> Yeah?

> OLIVE (V.O.)
> Do you think there's a heaven?

> FRANK (V.O.)
> That's hard to say, Olive. I don't
> think anyone knows for sure.

> OLIVE (V.O.)
> I know, but... What do you think?

> FRANK (V.O.)
> Um... Well...

> OLIVE (V.O.)
> (hesitates)
> I think there is a heaven.

> FRANK (V.O.)
> You think I'll get in?

> OLIVE (V.O.)
> Yes!

STILLS

Left to right: Toni Collette, Abigail Breslin, Alan Arkin, Paul Dano, Steve Carell, and Greg Kinnear. (All photos by Eric Lee.)

"There's no sense in entering a contest if you don't think you're going to win, so . . ."

" . . .Are you gonna win?" Greg Kinnear, *Richard*

My favorite shot from the whole movie.

Alan Arkin, *Grandpa*

Paul Dano, *Dwayne*

Abigail Breslin, *Olive*

Steve Carell, *Uncle Frank*

"Olive—you are the most beautiful girl in the whole world."

"Olive, Richard is an idiot."

The Hoover family.

Frank suffers another humiliation.

Steve and Toni, in action.

"Divorce! Bankrupt! Suicide! You're losers!"

The Hoover family—united at last.

Greg Kinnear, Toni Collette, Abigail Breslin, Steve Carell, and Beth Grant as *Pageant Official Nancy Jenkins*

Toni Collette, *Sheryl*

Directors Valerie Faris and Jonathan Dayton

Two of the best directors a writer could hope for.

Valerie Faris and Jonathan Dayton at work.

The directors intent on a scene.

Little Miss Sunshine

                         FRANK (V.O.)
             You promise?

                         OLIVE (V.O.)
             Yes!!!

                                              FADE TO BLACK

78   INT. VW BUS - ON THE ROAD - DAY   78

     They are cruising. Olive has her headphones back on, though
     she's not bouncing anymore -- just nodding her head. Sheryl
     points to a passing sign, "Redondo Beach -- 61 Miles."

                         SHERYL
             Sixty one miles. What time is it?

     Frank checks his watch.

                         FRANK
             Five of two...!

     Sheryl looks worriedly at Richard. Richard steps on the gas.

                         RICHARD
             We'll make it! Don't worry!

                         SHERYL
             We're cutting it close...

                         RICHARD
             It's not even close! We'll be...

     A car cuts in front of him. He brakes.

                         RICHARD (cont'd)
             Look out! Asshole!

     He HONKS the horn loudly at the guy.

                         FRANK
             What happened?

                         RICHARD
             He cut me off!

     The horn keeps HONKING intermittently.

                         SHERYL
             Okay. You can stop.

                         RICHARD
             It's not me! This thing is stuck.

He tries to pull the horn button up. Instead, he gets a long
continuous HOOOONK. He lets go. It stops.

                    SHERYL
          Okay, just leave it...!

Silence. Then a HONK. Another silence. HONK, HONK.

                    SHERYL (cont'd)
          Maybe if you pull it from...

She tries to lift up another part. HOOOONK. She stops.

                    RICHARD
          Just leave it, okay? We'll fix it
          when we get there!

                    SHERYL
          Okay, fine!

Silence. HONK! Silence. HONK! HONK! Silence. Dwayne
puts his head in his hands. He can't stand it. Frank
notices.

                    FRANK
          Maybe I can adopt you.

Dwayne stares out the window. HONK! Silence. HOOOONK!

79   EXT. HIGHWAY - DAY   79

The van, its horn BLARING, cruises past a State Trooper on
the side of the road. The TROOPER hits the lights.

80   INT. VW BUS - ON THE ROAD - DAY   80

Richard sees the lights in the rear-view mirror.

                    RICHARD
          Oh, Jesus! I'm being pulled over!
          Everybody: pretend to be normal, okay?
          Like everything is normal. Here we go...

He pulls onto the breakdown lane and stops. The HORN
continues HONKING intermittently. The Trooper, a 50-ish
California Highway Patrolman, gets out and approaches. His
tag reads, Sgt. McCleary.

                    OFFICER MCCLEARY
          How're you folks doin' today?

                    RICHARD
          Fine! Doin' fine!
                    (HONK)
          Sorry!

>   OFFICER McCLEARY
>   Having trouble with your horn?

>   RICHARD
>   Yeah, a little trouble.
>   (HONK)
>   Sorry!
>   (HONK)
>   Sorry!!!

Frank leans forward gleefully:

>   FRANK
>   Don't apologize, Rich! It's a sign
>   of weakness!

Richard ignores him.

>   OFFICER McCLEARY
>   Would you step out of your vehicle?

81   EXT. HIGHWAY - DAY   81

Reluctantly, Richard gets out. McCleary gestures towards the
back of the van.

>   OFFICER McCLEARY
>   Would you step this way?

>   RICHARD
>   No...!

>   OFFICER McCLEARY
>   What?

>   RICHARD
>   Don't...!

>   OFFICER McCLEARY
>   Don't what?

Richard shuts up. McCleary sees him glance at the trunk.

>   OFFICER McCLEARY (cont'd)
>   You have something in your trunk?

>   RICHARD
>   No! Nothing! It's just... Don't open
>   it.

McCleary is incredulous.

                    OFFICER MCCLEARY
          Sir, you realize you've just given
          me probable cause to search your
          trunk? Put your hands on top of
          your vehicle. Now don't move.

He shakes his head and walks back towards the trunk.

                    RICHARD
          Please! It's not illegal, it's...

                    OFFICER MCCLEARY
          Sir, I'd advise you to keep your
          mouth shut.

Richard shuts up. McCleary pulls his gun and hesitantly
approaches the trunk.

82   INT. VW BUS - DAY   82

Everyone surreptitiously watches.

                    SHERYL
               (sotto)
          Oh no, what's he doing?! Oh god!

83   EXT. HIGHWAY - DAY   83

Richard watches McCleary walk around the back of the bus. He
closes his eyes. McCleary opens the trunk.

                    OFFICER MCCLEARY
          Whoa! Goddamn!!!

Richard opens his eyes, shakes his head -- this is the end.

                    OFFICER McCLEARY (cont'd)
          Sir, would you come here?

Richard walks back. McCleary bends down behind the bus.

Rounding the corner, Richard sees McCleary picking up
Grandpa's porn magazines, which have spilled onto the road.

The bundled sheet sits in plain sight. McCleary, distracted,
gathers the magazines and stands. He grins.

                    OFFICER McCLEARY (cont'd)
          Don't worry, I won't bust you.

He looks in the bus, smiles and waves at Sheryl and Olive.

84   INT. VW BUS - DAY   84

Everyone in the bus -- minds blown -- waves back.

85 EXT. HIGHWAY - DAY   85

McCleary tidies the magazines and, grinning, shuffles through
them with a connoisseur's eye -- Swank, High Society, Black
Tail. The next magazine: Honcho.

A beefy, moustached stud gazes smolderingly from the cover.

McCleary stops grinning. He looks at Richard. Richard
shrugs and laughs nervously.

86 INT. VW BUS - DAY   86

As the Trooper's cruiser pulls back onto the highway,
Richard walks to the front, climbs in, slams the door.

                    SHERYL
          What happened?!

                    RICHARD
          I'll tell you when I regain
          consciousness.
                    (starts the car)
          Frank. Dwayne. Get out and push.

87 INT. VW BUS - ON THE ROAD - DAY   87

They are cruising. The horn HONKS in occasional spurts.
Everyone ignores it. Olive plays with an eye chart she got
at the hospital. She points at a diminishing set of "E"s.

Dwayne is in the back seat, holding a hand over one eye and
pointing his finger up, down, or sideways to correspond to
the rotation of the "E". Dwayne makes it through the chart.

                    OLIVE
          20/20 vision! Mom, Dwayne has
          20/20 vision!

                    SHERYL
          I bet he does.

                    OLIVE
          Okay, further back!

Dwayne and Olive continue with the charts, with Dwayne
sitting further back. Sheryl points to a passing sign.

                    SHERYL
          There! Redondo Beach! Forty six!

Frank checks his watch.

                    FRANK
          It's 2:15...!

Sheryl looks at Richard, who steps on the gas.

                    RICHARD
          We'll make it, okay?! Maybe a few
          minutes late.

                    SHERYL
          No, Richard...! They said three
          o'clock sharp! They were very
          explicit. You don't want to cross
          these people. Trust me.

                    FRANK
          You know where it is?

                    SHERYL
          The Holiday Inn. She said it's just off
          the highway. You can't miss it.

                    RICHARD
          She better be right.

In the back, Olive pulls out a new flyer.

                    OLIVE
          Okay, now I'm gonna test if you're
          colorblind. What letter is in the
          circle?

She holds up a chart with a green circle. Inside the circle,
in a mosaic pattern, is a bright red letter "A". Dwayne
makes a gesture, "There's nothing there."

                    OLIVE (cont'd)
          No, inside the circle! Right there!

Dwayne shakes his head again. Olive glances at Frank.

                    OLIVE (cont'd)
          It's an "A"! Can't you see it?!
          It's red! See? Right there!

Dwayne takes the chart and stares at it.

                    FRANK
          You can't see the "A"? It's bright
          red. Can you see the difference
          between the green and the red?

Dwayne shakes his head helplessly. Frank turns away.

                    FRANK (cont'd)
          Oh, man.

Dwayne looks at him. He pulls out his pad and writes:

"What?"

Frank doesn't say anything. Dwayne points violently at the
pad. Frank looks at him. Quietly:

                    FRANK (cont'd)
          Dwayne. I think you're colorblind.

Dwayne doesn't understand. He points at the pad again.

                    FRANK (cont'd)
          You can't fly jets if you're
          colorblind.

Dwayne does nothing. Then he seems to implode in on himself,
curling up in a ball. Frank shouts towards the front.

                    FRANK (cont'd)
          Rich, pull over!

                    RICHARD
          What?!

                    FRANK
          We have an emergency back here!

                    RICHARD
          What is it?

                    FRANK
          Just pull over!

                    RICHARD
          What's the emergency?

                    FRANK
          Sheryl, will you make him pull over?!

                    SHERYL
          Richard!!!

                    RICHARD
          I'm pulling over, okay?! I'm
          pulling over!

He puts on the clicker.

88   EXT. SIDE OF THE INTERSTATE - DAY   88

The bus pulls into the break-down lane beside the highway.

The door slides open and Dwayne gets out onto the grassy
slope by the side of the road. He walks off with his head in
his hands. This is the first time we've heard his voice.

                    DWAYNE
          Fuck!!!
                    (beat)
          Fuck!!!

The others get out of the car and watch him.

                    SHERYL
          What happened?

                    FRANK
          He's colorblind. He can't fly.

                    SHERYL
          Oh, Jesus. Oh, no.

Thirty yards away Dwayne falls to his knees, buries his hands
and face in the grass, and SHRIEKS like a wild animal.

There's an out-of-control quality to his behavior that is
scary and disturbing. Finally, Dwayne rolls to a sitting
position, hands covering his face. He sits there crying.

The others don't know what to do. Richard glances at Sheryl.
He points at his watch.

                    SHERYL (cont'd)
          Let's give him a second.

In the background, the VW keeps HONKING like some demonic
beast -- mocking Dwayne's helplessness.

Finally, Sheryl approaches Dwayne.

                    SHERYL (cont'd)
          Dwayne? Honey? I'm sorry.

He says nothing. She sighs.

                    SHERYL (cont'd)
          Dwayne... Come on, we gotta go.

                    DWAYNE
          I'm not going.

                    SHERYL
          Dwayne...

                    DWAYNE
          I'm not! I don't care! I'm not
          getting in that bus again!

                    SHERYL
          Dwayne... For better or worse:
          we're your family...

Dwayne stands up and screams at them.

                    DWAYNE
          You're not my family! I don't want
          to be your family! I hate you
          fucking people! I hate you!
                    (he points at them)
          Divorce! Bankrupt! Suicide!
          You're losers! You're fucking
          losers!

Everyone is stunned by this outburst. Dwayne puts his hands
over his eyes and sits down again.

                    DWAYNE (cont'd)
          Just leave me, Mom. Please? Just
          leave me here.

Sheryl gets up and walks back to the others.

                    SHERYL
          I don't know what to do.

                    RICHARD
          We're gonna be late. Can we leave
          somebody here with him?

                    FRANK
          I'll stay.

                    SHERYL
          No, we're not doing that.

                    RICHARD
          Olive, you want to talk to him?

                    SHERYL
          No, Richard. There's nothing to
          say. We just have to wait.

A beat. Then Olive walks over and sits down next to Dwayne.

Dwayne's face is red and snot is dribbling from his nose. He
has a piece of straw and he's poking some ants in the grass.

She puts her arm on his shoulder and watches him poke. The
ants climb busily over the grass. They sit quietly.

Then Dwayne stands up.

                    DWAYNE
          Okay, let's go.

He walks back to the others. His voice is automatic.

DWAYNE (cont'd)
I apologize for the things I said.
I was upset. I didn't really mean
them.

FRANK
(mock-tender)
Dwayne... We know you did.

SHERYL
Frank...
(to Dwayne)
It's okay. Let's just go.

They all start pushing the bus.

89   INT. VW BUS - ON THE ROAD - DAY   89

Richard is weaving through traffic -- the engine's REVVING
VERY HIGH. Richard, Sheryl, Olive, and Frank are looking
ahead intently. Dwayne is slouched in the back, staring at
nothing. The horn has tapered off to an occasional HONK.

Frank checks his watch.

FRANK
2:50...!

RICHARD
We're gonna make it! Olive, don't
worry! We'll be on time!

JUMP TO:

The same. Frank checks his watch.

FRANK
2:55!

RICHARD
Just look for the exit! It's
coming up!

JUMP TO:

The same. Frank checks his watch again.

FRANK
2:58!

No one says anything. Then Richard points.

RICHARD
There! That's it! Can anyone see
a Holiday Inn?

A beat. Olive points.

>   OLIVE
>   There! Little Miss Sunshine!

As they ride up the exit ramp, the sign in front of the
Holiday Inn reads, "Little Miss Sunshine."

Richard comes off the ramp onto a four lane commercial road.

There's a maze of service roads and parking lots between him
and the Holiday Inn. Richard is baffled.

>   RICHARD
>   How the fuck do you get over there?

>   SHERYL
>   Turn here! Turn here!

Richard takes a right into a service road.

>   SHERYL (cont'd)
>   Will you slow down?

>   RICHARD
>   I can't! I'm in third gear!

>   FRANK
>   2:59!

>   RICHARD
>   Does anyone see a turn-off? How
>   the fuck do you get over there?

They drive past the Holiday Inn -- a few hundred yards away.

>   OLIVE
>   Dad! You drove past it!

>   RICHARD
>   There's no place to turn in!

>   SHERYL
>   Turn around! You gotta turn around!

>   RICHARD
>   Okay, hold on, everybody.

The VW screeches around in a wide arc across four lanes of
(luckily empty) traffic. Richard guns the under-revving
engine. They again drive past the distant Holiday Inn.

>   RICHARD (cont'd)
>   Can anyone see a way in?

                         SHERYL
          Go over there, then cut across!

                         RICHARD
          Okay, hold on!

The VW squeals around a left turn onto another service road.

                         RICHARD (cont'd)
          There's no way in! What the fuck?!

                         OLIVE
          Dad! You're driving past it!

                         SHERYL
          There! Into the parking lot!

She points. Richard turns into an enormous empty parking
lot. He drives towards the Holiday Inn in the distance.

There's still no clear path on how to get there.

                         RICHARD
          It's a dead end!

                         SHERYL
          No, go over there!

                         RICHARD
          It's the same! There's no way...!

He turns the wheel and they begin tracing a wide loop --
bombing around the parking lot at 35 mph in a holding
pattern. Frank looks at his watch. With quiet finality:

                         FRANK
          Three o'clock.

                         OLIVE
          Dad...!

                         SHERYL
          Go back out!

                         RICHARD
          We tried that! There's no way in!

                         SHERYL
          So we just keep going in circles?

Richard says nothing. Finally:

                         RICHARD
          Okay: Hold on, everybody! Olive,
          put your seat belt on.

He comes out of a wide arc and heads straight for the median strips separating him from the Holiday Inn.

                    SHERYL
          Oh, my God!

                    RICHARD
          Hold on, everyone!

He guns it. As soon as he hits the first median, the HORN goes off and doesn't stop. They're in a new parking lot.

                    SHERYL
          Look out!

Richard goes SCREECHING past several parked cars. They're one median strip away from the Holiday Inn parking lot.

                    RICHARD
          One more! Here we go! Hold on!

They hit the median hard. A big bump. They've made it into the Holiday Inn parking lot. The whole van sags to the rear.

Frank looks out the rear window.

A tire is wheeling off across the parking lot by itself.

                    FRANK
          We lost a tire, Rich!

                    RICHARD
          We'll get it later! Here we go!

They come gliding into a parking space, HORN BLARING.

Frank yanks open the sliding door. It slides back, slams into the end of the track and derails. The whole door falls off the side of the van and into the parking lot.

Frank doesn't even look back. He sprints across the lot towards a distant banner marked "Little Miss Sunshine."

All the others -- except Dwayne -- sprint after him.

90   INT. HOTEL ENTRANCE - DAY   90

A big carpeted hotel lobby. The doors open and Frank comes in, breathless. He stops.

90A   INT. REGISTRATION HALL - DAY   90A

The place is crowded with tiny blond girls and their mothers. The girls are dressed, coiffed and made-up to perfection.

Nearby, a CONTEST OFFICIAL is packing up a table with a
"Registration" banner. Frank sprints up to her. The others
catch up and stand, looking on -- desperate, dishevelled,
breathing hard. Her name tag reads "Nancy Jenkins, Director."

                    FRANK
          Hi, we're here to register!

                    MS. JENKINS
          Sorry, we're closed.

                    FRANK
          But we have an entrant. Right
          here. We just need to check in.

                    MS. JENKINS
          Registration ended at three.

                    FRANK
          It's three now!

                    MS. JENKINS
          No...

She points to a clock on the wall. It's 3:04 PM.

                    RICHARD
          Oh, have a heart! We're four
          minutes late! We just drove all
          the way from Albuquerque...!

                    MS. JENKINS
          Then you should have been here by
          three.

She tries to leave. Richard stops her.

                    RICHARD
          Wait, wait, wait! How can we make
          this work?

                    MS. JENKINS
          Everyone else was here before three. I'd
          be giving unfair advantage...

                    RICHARD
          We're not asking for an advantage!
          We just want to compete!

                    MS. JENKINS
          Don't yell at me, sir. I didn't make you
          late. We've settled on the schedule of
          the show and we've turned off our
          computers.
                    (MORE)

                    MS. JENKINS (cont'd)
          Now our line-up is finalized, I have a
          hair check to do, I'm sorry you're late,
          but I can't help you.

She tries to leave but they block her way. Richard gets on
his knees.

                    RICHARD
          Please! You don't know what we've
          been through...!

                    SOUND GUY (O.S.)
          Uh, Ms. Jenkins...?

They all turn. There's a SOUND GUY -- a very portly young
man with a high voice -- who's just heard the story.

                    SOUND GUY (cont'd)
          I can put 'em in the system.

                    MS. JENKINS
          Oh, Kirby, you don't have to!

                    KIRBY
          No, it's okay. It's five minutes.

                    MS. JENKINS
          Well... It's your time. 'Scuse me.

She pushes past them. Frank leaps up.

                    FRANK
          Hello! Everyone?! We've just
          witnessed a great act of compassion
          and human kindness! Exhibit A:
          we've got Eva Braun here -- making
          the trains run on time -- and B:
          Kirby! My man! Currently the
          greatest human on the planet!
          Applause, please!

He leads the others in applause. Everyone in the lobby
ignores them. Kirby smiles, flips on the computer. They
crowd around.

                    SHERYL
          Thank you so much! You don't know
          what this means...

                    KIRBY
          Please. It's five minutes.

He glances in the direction of Ms. Jenkins, who has departed,
and shakes his head. Quietly:

                              KIRBY (cont'd)
          I ain't working for these people
          again. These people are crazy.
                    (to Olive)
          So, what's your name?

                              OLIVE
          Olive.

                              KIRBY
          Olive. That's a nice name.

She smiles. He starts tapping away at the computer.

Olive glances away and freezes. Across the room is Miss
California, sitting behind a table, signing photos for kids.
Olive is in awe.

                              OLIVE
          Mom! It's Miss California! Look!
          It's really her!

                              SHERYL
          You want to say hello?

Olive shakes her head, intimidated -- it's like meeting a god.

                              SHERYL (cont'd)
          Come on, she looks nice. We'll
          just say hi, okay?

Olive nods, transfixed by the sight of Miss California.

Frank -- having slipped away -- rejoins the group and
brandishes a crisp new Sunday New York Times at Sheryl.

                              FRANK
          Score, baby! Jackpot!

                              SHERYL
          Okay, fine. Just don't forget
          about the contest.

She notices Dwayne -- still shut-down -- standing forlornly
at the edge of the group.

                              SHERYL (cont'd)
          Dwayne, honey, I know you hate all
          of us, but since we're here anyway,
          why don't you guys go to the beach?

                              FRANK
          Hey, there's an idea! The beach!
          C'mon, we'll walk over, go surfing.
                    (MORE)

                    FRANK (cont'd)
          Maybe meet some chicks. Whaddaya
          say?

Dwayne -- indifferent -- turns and walks off. Sheryl watches
him go, turns to Frank -- at a loss. Frank gestures -- I'm
on it -- and follows after Dwayne. Sheryl watches him go --
somewhat reassured -- and turns to Richard.

                    RICHARD
              (re: Miss California)
          Go on. I got this.

Sheryl nods, takes Olive's hand and leads her to the back of
the line -- a half a dozen girls and mothers. The GIRL in
front of them turns and stares -- sizing up the competition.

Olive smiles.

                    OLIVE
          Hi...!

The Girl quickly turns back around, not saying anything.

Olive takes this in stride. She turns and looks around the
room at the other girls. They are all primped to perfection.

Olive is still dressed in her traveling clothes -- denim cut-
offs and black Converse high-tops. She stands out.

Two TWIN GIRLS are chasing each other around, giggling.

Olive watches. Eventually, the Twins see Olive watching them.

They whisper to each other and giggle. Olive gives them a
friendly half-smile. Finally, the Twin Girls approach Olive.

                    TWIN GIRL ONE
          Are you on a diet?

                    OLIVE
          What?

                    TWIN GIRL ONE
          Are you on a diet?

                    OLIVE
          No...!

                    TWIN GIRL TWO
          Didn't think so!

They dissolve into giggles and run away. Olive is disturbed.

Sheryl is steamed but doesn't know what to do.

ACROSS THE ROOM

Kirby finishes up with Richard -- having him sign a release --
and hands him a goody bag filled with pageant materials.

> KIRBY
> And sign...
> (Richard signs)
> ...And you're done! Here's your
> receipt; tickets; sash; tiara.
> Anything else?

> RICHARD
> Yeah. Is there a funeral home
> around here?

91   ACROSS THE ROOM   91

Dwayne approaches a far corner of the room where a couple of
overstuffed wing-back chairs sit empty. He slouches into a
chair and half-covers his eyes -- trying to block out the
world. Off-screen we HEAR NOISE of pre-pageant preparations.

CLOSE ON -- Dwayne, trying to understand his life.

DWAYNE'S POV -- Through BLURRY FINGERS there's nothing but
floral wallpaper, wall-to-wall carpeting, and a potted plant.

Dwayne looks over. Frank approaches, carrying his NY Times.

> FRANK
> Hey. Mind if I join you?

Dwayne turns away, facing the other way.

Frank looks at Dwayne. There's nothing to be done. He
settles into the other chair, pulls out his NY Times.

> FRANK (cont'd)
> So look, I know you're crazy for
> the Arts & Leisure, but... I put
> out the bucks and you're just gonna
> have to wait.

No response. He opens up the Sunday New York Times.

> FRANK (cont'd)
> Sorry.

He looks at Dwayne for a beat, then shakes his head and opens
up the Book Review section.

IN THE BOOK REVIEW

is a full-page ad for Understanding Proust by Larry Sugarman.

A banner reads, "The Surprise Best-Seller from America's # 1
Proust Scholar!" There's a photo of Larry Sugarman, in a
beard and glasses, looking very serious.

Frank stares at the ad.

92   OMIT   92

93   EXT. PARKING LOT - DAY   93

Richard approaches the VW bus with two funeral home WORKERS
in jumpsuits who affect a bored, seen-it-all demeanor.

WORKER ONE, 40s, is an old pro. WORKER TWO, 20s, is a fresh-
faced rookie. A FUNERAL HOME VAN is parked in the background.

                    RICHARD
          ...We're driving five, six hours --
          we thought he was napping. By the
          time we figured it out it was...

                    WORKER ONE
          ...Too late. So where's the body?

Richard turns, pops the trunk, averts his eyes, and opens it.
The Workers look in the trunk. Then look at Richard.

94   INT. REGISTRATION HALL - DAY   94

Olive finally makes it to the front of the line.

                    MISS CALIFORNIA
          Hi! What's your name?

                    OLIVE
          Olive.

                    MISS CALIFORNIA
          What's your talent, Olive?

                    OLIVE
          I like dancing!

                    MISS CALIFORNIA
          Dancing? Dancing was too hard for
          me! I'm a singer. You must be a
          good dancer!

                    OLIVE
          I am! I'm really good!

                    MISS CALIFORNIA
          I bet you are! Well, thanks for
          stopping by, Olive. Best of luck!

But Olive is not quite ready to move on.

                    OLIVE
Ummm... Miss California?

                    MISS CALIFORNIA
You can call me Bonnie!

                    OLIVE
Bonnie...? Do you eat ice cream?

                    MISS CALIFORNIA
                        (perplexed)
Yes! I love ice cream! My
favorite flavor is Chocolate Cherry
Garcia. Although, technically, I
think that's a frozen yogurt.
Okay?

                    OLIVE
Okay, thank you, Bonnie! Bye!

                    MISS CALIFORNIA
Bye!
                        (to the next girl)
Hi, what's your name?

Sheryl and Olive head off.

                    OLIVE
She eats ice cream, Mom!

                    SHERYL
I heard!

95   EXT. PARKING LOT - DAY   95

Richard signs an invoice. Worker Two closes the rear doors
of the van, climbs in the driver's seat, starts the engine.

Richard hands the clipboard to Worker One. He hands Richard
a small cardboard box.

                    WORKER ONE
The personal effects...

                    RICHARD
Oh. Thank you.

                    WORKER ONE
You take care.

                         RICHARD
              You too. Thanks.

Worker One gets in the van and slams the door.

The van pulls out, drives to the edge of the parking lot and
puts on its turn signal. Richard watches. The van pulls
into the street and drives off, disappearing into traffic.

Richard is left alone.

96   EXT. PAGEANT DRESSING ROOM, OLIVE'S STATION - DAY   96

Sheryl and Olive hurry past one little girl after another --
each being made up to perfection by her Mom or a Groomer.

Hair is teased; eye shadow is applied; tans are sprayed on.

All the make-up tables seem taken. Finally, Sheryl finds an
empty table in the corner. She pulls out a bathing suit.

                         SHERYL
              Okay, Olive. Let's put on your
              swimsuit. Here. You want to
              change behind the curtain?

Olive takes the swim-suit and heads for the changing area as
Sheryl begins rapidly unpacking up Olive's costumes.

A clipboard-carrying, headset-wearing Pageant Assistant --
name tag: Pam -- leans into the room and calls out.

                         PAM
              Last touch-ups, everyone! Last
              touch-ups!

96A   OMIT   96A

96B   OMIT   96B

97   INT. PRIVATE CHANGING AREA - DAY   97

Olive finishes putting on her swim-suit. There's a full-
length mirror in the changing area.

Olive turns around and reaches for the curtain. She stops.

She steps back and looks at herself in the mirror.

She turns sideways. She sucks her stomach in.

This is the first time she's ever done this.

Olive turns back frontal. She lets her stomach hang out.

She's not happy with what she sees -- also the first time.

98   INT. PAGEANT DRESSING ROOM - DAY   98

Sheryl finishes gathering up Olive's costumes.

                         SHERYL
               Olive, you ready?

                    OLIVE (O.S.)
          Coming!

99   INT. PRIVATE CHANGING AREA - DAY   99

Olive stares at herself in the mirror. She's making up her
mind about something. (Winner or Loser?)

Then, very determined, she walks out of the changing area.

100 INT. PAGEANT DRESSING ROOM, OLIVE'S STATION - DAY   100

Olive comes out of the changing area. Sheryl is at the make-
up table, ready for action.

                         SHERYL
               Okay, we have about one minute.
               You want to do hair or make-up?

Olive thinks. It's like the fate of the free world is at
stake. Finally:

                         OLIVE
               Make-up...!

Kirby approaches, in a rush.

                         KIRBY
               Hey...! I need your music!

Olive goes to her bag, digs in, hands him a disc.

                         OLIVE
               Here.

                         KIRBY
               This? Did you choose this?

                         OLIVE
               My Grandpa did.

                         KIRBY
               Your Grandpa? What track?

                         OLIVE
               Twelve. Oh, one thing...?

She glances at Sheryl, then goes and whispers in Kirby's ear.
Kirby smiles.

                    KIRBY
          Okay! I'll be looking for you.

                    OLIVE
          Thank you, Kirby!

He hurries off.

100A OMIT   100A

101   INT. REGISTRATION HALL - DAY   101

Dwayne slumps in his chair, facing the corner. Frank sits in
his chair, staring at nothing. A confederacy of misery.

Abruptly, Dwayne sits up, looks at Frank. He's depressed,
but no longer catatonic. Frank glances over. A beat.

Dwayne stands, heads for a side exit.

                    DWAYNE
          Let's get out of here.

ACROSS THE ROOM

Richard enters the hall through the main entrance -- holding
the box of Grandpa's stuff -- finds a bench and sits.

He seems shaken. Around him, the crowd in the lobby has
thinned out as people line up to enter the auditorium.
Across the room, Sheryl and Olive step out of a double door,
survey the lobby, and spot Richard sitting alone. Holding
hands, they rush across the floor to him. Richard looks up.

                    SHERYL
          We need the sash and the tiara!

Richard nods. He locates the goody bag that Kirby gave him
and hands it to Sheryl. Sheryl turns to go. He stops them.

                    RICHARD
          Wait a sec. Olive, come here. Time for a
          pep talk.

                    SHERYL
          Richard, we can't...!

                    RICHARD
          This is important! Olive, come here.

She goes to him. He hunches down, takes her hand.

                              RICHARD (cont'd)
                    Now I know you and Grandpa worked on
                    this together. I know how much it
                    meant to him. We drove nine hundred
                    miles to get here. Our car broke
                    down. We've been through a lot...

He hesitates, searching for words as if the very meaning of
his life were at stake. He falters. When he finally speaks,
it's with a bare, at-the-end-of-his-rope nakedness.

                              RICHARD (cont'd)
                    Olive, if there's one thing in this
                    life I know is true, it's this: We
                    live in a world that only cares
                    about winners...

                              SHERYL
                    Richard...! Jesus! Come on, Olive!

She tries to pull Olive away, but Richard holds on.

                              RICHARD
                    Okay, Olive? Okay...?

Olive stares at him. Finally, she nods. Richard lets go.

Sheryl pulls Olive away, and they rush off towards the
backstage area. Richard watches them go.

102   OMIT   102

103   OMIT   103

104   INT. AUDITORIUM - DAY   104

Richard finds his reserved seats -- four seats on the aisle.
He sits in the fourth seat and lays his jacket across the
other three, saving them for Sheryl, Dwayne, and Frank.

The guy one seat over is a grizzled BIKER sitting impassively
with his arms folded. Richard tries to be friendly.

                              RICHARD
                    Hey.

The Biker glances at him and nods. Richard persists.

                              RICHARD (cont'd)
                    You got a kid in the show?

The Biker looks at him. He takes an earplug out of his ear.

                              BIKER
                    What?

                         RICHARD
              You got a kid in the show?

The Biker stares at him.

                         BIKER
                   First time?

Richard nods -- Yeah! The Biker nods -- Figures. He puts
the earplug back in his ear and resumes his impassive stare.

Richard is unnerved. The LIGHTS DIM.

Onstage, an MC steps up to a microphone. A DRUMROLL.

                         MC
              Ladies and gentlemen. Welcome to
              the 24th annual Little Miss
              Sunshine pageant! Let's welcome
              the contestants!

MUSIC. Big APPLAUSE.

Twenty-five little girls parade out on stage in swim-suits.
Twenty of them are blond -- some bleached. They've been
arranged from shortest to tallest.

Olive -- at least two inches taller than everyone else -- is
at the end of the line.

The girls parade around in a loop, waving and smiling.

They end up in a line running across the stage.

                         MC (cont'd)
              We have twenty five contestants
              from all over the State of
              California. At the end of the
              evening, one of these girls will be
              crowned Little Miss Sunshine!

Richard, in the audience, claps enthusiastically. The Biker
claps without enthusiasm.

105   EXT. BEACH - AFTERNOON   105

      A glorious, sunny day. The ocean stretches to infinity.

      Dwayne and Frank, in swim trunks, carry surfboards marked
      "Southcoast Surf Shop" to the edge of the beach. The ocean's
      dead calm. Dwayne looks out at the water.

                         DWAYNE
              There's no waves, Frank.

                    FRANK
          We don't need waves. We'll just
          paddle out.

106   INT. AUDITORIUM - DAY   106

      The MC is up on the stage. Another DRUMROLL.

                    MC
          ...Let's hear a big round of
          applause for the evening wear!

      MUSIC. Big APPLAUSE. The same girls -- in precocious
      evening-wear -- come out in the same order and do the same
      little loop around the stage. Olive's on the end again.

      Richard, in the crowd, applauds -- a little less heartily.

107   EXT. ON THE WATER - DAY   107

      Frank and Dwayne paddle straight out into the ocean. It's
      calm, but the shore is a long way away. Dwayne looks back.

                    DWAYNE
          How far are we?

                    FRANK
          I dunno. Quarter mile?

                    DWAYNE
          You wanna stop?

      Frank shrugs. They stop. Frank looks down into the water.

                    FRANK
          Hey. Think you can touch bottom?

                    DWAYNE
          How far is it?

                    FRANK
          I dunno. Must be ten, twelve feet at
          least. Come on! Y'ready? On your mark,
          get set...

      They dive down into the water, disappearing.

      The two surfboards drift aimlessly, side by side.

      Dwayne resurfaces, breathing hard, grabs his board. He looks
      around. Nothing. He cranes his neck.

      No sign of Frank. Dwayne frowns. He shields his eyes and
      tries to look through the water with increasing urgency.

Abruptly, Frank surfaces ten yards behind him.

> FRANK (cont'd)
> Ahhh, gotcha!

Dwayne turns and smiles -- relieved. It is perhaps the first unguarded smile we've seen from him.

Forgetting himself, he dives back into the water.

108	OMIT	108
109	OMIT	109
110	OMIT	110
111	INT. AUDITORIUM - DAY	111

The MC is up on stage. Another DRUMROLL.

> MC
> And now! The moment you've been waiting for! The talent competition! Ladies and gentleman, please welcome Amber Tiffany Harper, who'll be singing a tune from the Broadway show, "Annie." Amber!

A little girl walks out -- very stagy -- and begins to sing:

> AMBER
> "The sun'll come out...tomorrow..."

Richard sits in the audience. He's growing uneasy.

| 112 | EXT. ON THE WATER - DAY | 112 |

They sit on their boards and look out to sea.

> FRANK
> Man, it's beautiful out here.
> (beat)
> I don't know if I believe in God, but the ocean -- it's always here for you: infinitely bigger than you are, and completely indifferent. So... My version of God.

> DWAYNE
> Frank...?
> (Frank looks over)
> What was it like when you cut your wrists?

Frank takes a breath.

> FRANK
> You know, I wish I could tell you I
> felt bad. But I didn't. I was...
> Outside the world, y'know? It was
> very peaceful.
> (beat)
> But, I'm feeling that way now, too, so...

He shrugs. Dwayne nods. He looks out to sea.

> DWAYNE
> Sometimes I wish I could just go to
> sleep until I was eighteen. Just
> skip all this crap -- high school
> and everything. Just skip it...

He shakes his head.

> FRANK
> Y'ever hear of Marcel Proust?

> DWAYNE
> He's the guy you teach?

> FRANK
> Yeah. French writer. Total loser.
> Never had a real job. Unrequited
> love affairs. Gay. Spent twenty
> years writing a book almost no one
> reads. But...he was also probably
> the greatest writer since
> Shakespeare. Anyway, he gets down
> to the end of his life, he looks
> back and he decides that all the
> years he suffered -- those were the
> best years of his life. Because
> they made him who he was. They
> forced him to think and grow, and
> to feel very deeply. And the years
> he was happy? Total waste. Didn't
> learn anything.

Dwayne grins.

> FRANK (cont'd)
> So, if you sleep til you're
> eighteen...
> (scoffs)
> ...Think of the suffering you'd
> miss! High school's your prime
> suffering years. You don't get
> better suffering than that!
> (MORE)

                         FRANK (cont'd)
          Unless you go into academia, but
          that's a whole different story.

They share a smile. Dwayne gazes out to sea. A beat.

                         DWAYNE
          You know what...?
               (Frank looks over)
          Fuck beauty contests. Life is one
          fucking beauty contest after
          another. School, then college,
          then work. Fuck it. Fuck the Air
          Force Academy. Fuck the MacArthur
          Foundation. If I want to fly, I'll
          find a way to fly. You do what you
          love and fuck the rest.

Frank stares at Dwayne, impressed. Dwayne glances at Frank,
who tries to play it cool.

                         FRANK
          I'm glad you're talking again,
          Dwayne. You're not nearly as
          stupid as you look.

Dwayne smiles. Frank looks around.

                         FRANK (cont'd)
          So now what do we do?

                         DWAYNE
          You got me, Frank. Maybe we can
          stay out here forever.

A beat. They look at each other.

                         FRANK
          Wanna go in?

                         DWAYNE
          Yah. We should go.

They begin paddling back to shore.

113   INT. AUDITORIUM - DAY   113

A tiny girl in a COWGIRL outfit -- smiling like crazy -- taps
her way through a tap-dance routine. She's fantastic.

Richard's smile is fading. He's starting to worry.

114   EXT. BOARDWALK - DAY   114

Frank exits a T-shirt shop and throws a shirt to Dwayne.

                              FRANK
                 I can't believe we found these. I
                 hope they fit.

As they stride up the boardwalk, he strips off his shirt and

puts on his new T-shirt. In big block letters, it says:

                    "LOSER"

Dwayne puts on his. It's the same. Frank looks at him.

                              FRANK (cont'd)
                 You're every mother's dream,
                 Dwayne. Come on.

They head off.

115   INT. AUDITORIUM - DAY   115

Another TINY BLONDE GIRL sings while flouncing and prancing
across the stage, blowing kisses and twirling a parasol. She
skips around the MC, flirting and batting her eyes.

The audience -- charmed -- starts clapping along. As she
finishes, the audience rises as one in a standing ovation.

Richard is the only one to remain seated. His face sinks as
reality finally hits him -- there's no way Olive will win.

He gets up and departs.

116   INT. REGISTRATION HALL - DAY   116

Frank and Dwayne enter and stride towards the doors of the
auditorium. They open the door and walk into a BLAST of
syrupy singing.

The door shuts. The door reopens. Frank and Dwayne stagger
out. They look at each other.

                              DWAYNE
                 I'm going backstage.

                              FRANK
                 Right. See ya.

Dwayne heads off as Frank leans against a wall, recovering.

117   INT. BACKSTAGE HALLWAY - DAY   117

Dwayne strides through the backstage, looking for Sheryl and
Olive. With his wet hair and LOSER T-shirt, he stands out.

The clipboard-carrying Assistant, Pam, tries to stop him.

> PAM
> Excuse me? You authorized to be
> backstage?

> DWAYNE
> No.

He continues walking. Everywhere there are little blond girls
crying, whining, or lolling about. The mothers are over-dressed,
over-coiffed, and over-stressed. It's intense.

He stops, turns to a little PRINCESS slouched on a sofa.

> DWAYNE (cont'd)
> Hey. Where are the dressing rooms?

> PRINCESS
> Are you allowed to be here?

> DWAYNE
> Just tell me where the dressing
> rooms are.

> PRINCESS
> (yelling off-screen)
> Mom...! Mom...!!!

Dwayne rolls his eyes, moves on.

118   OMIT   118

119   INT. PAGEANT DRESSING ROOM, OLIVE'S STATION - DAY   119

Richard wanders through the backstage. He spots Sheryl and
Olive in a small dressing room in the back. He approaches.

Olive is sitting in a make-up chair, wearing gold hot pants
and a red top. It's a slightly bizarre ensemble, given her
girlish plumpness. Richard hesitates. Sheryl sees him.

> SHERYL
> Hey. What's going on?

> RICHARD
> I came to wish Olive good luck.
> (to Olive)
> How're you doin'?

> OLIVE
> (weak)
> Good.

> SHERYL
> (sotto voce)
> Nervous.

                    RICHARD
        You're gonna do great! I know it!
                (to Sheryl)
        Can I talk to you a sec?

She nods. They wander a few steps out of Olive's hearing
range. Richard is agitated, troubled.

                    SHERYL
        What's up?

                    RICHARD
                (hesitates)
        I don't want Olive to go on.

                    SHERYL
                (can't believe it)
        Are you kidding...?!!!

                    RICHARD
        We're not in Albuquerque anymore, all
        right? She's out of her league here.

                    SHERYL
        So...?

                    RICHARD
        Sheryl...! She's not gonna win.
        There's no fucking way.

                    SHERYL
        It doesn't matter...!

                    RICHARD
        It does matter!

                    SHERYL
        It doesn't matter!

                    RICHARD
        It does!!!

Suddenly, all Richard's emotions rush to the surface.

                    RICHARD (cont'd)
        I don't want her to lose. I know
        what that feels like. It's not
        good. We can't let that happen.

She stares at him. It's the first time he's admitted to any
kind of vulnerability or weakness. She takes his hand.

                    SHERYL
        Richard...!

They look at each other. This is the first honest moment
we've seen between them.

Unfortunately, they are interrupted by Dwayne, who enters --
a determined look on his face. Sheryl sees him coming.

>   SHERYL (cont'd)
>   Hey. How're you feeling?!

>   DWAYNE
>   Better. Where's Olive?

>   SHERYL
>   In the dressing room. What's up?

>   DWAYNE
>   (hesitates, then sotto)
>   Mom, I don't want Olive doing this.

>   SHERYL
>   Oh, my God...!

>   RICHARD
>   See?!

>   DWAYNE
>   Look around! This place is fucked!
>   I don't want these people judging
>   Olive! Fuck them!

>   RICHARD
>   Exactly! Fuck them!

Dwayne glances at Richard, unnerved by his agreement.

>   SHERYL
>   No, Dwayne. It's too late...

>   DWAYNE
>   It's not too late! You're the Mom!
>   You're supposed to protect her!
>   (beat)
>   Everyone's gonna laugh at her, Mom.
>   Please don't let her do this.

Sheryl stares at him, wavering. The clipboard-wielding, head-
set wearing Pageant Assistant, Pam, passes by and calls out.

>   PAM
>   Olive Hoover! Two minutes.

She walks on. They watch her go. Dwayne and Sheryl face off.

>   DWAYNE
>   She's not a beauty queen, Mom...

120   INT. OLIVE'S STATION - DAY   120

       Olive stands, listening. Her face betrays nothing. Dwayne's
       VOICE is faint but clear.

                          DWAYNE (O.S.)
                   ...She's just not.

121   INT. PAGEANT DRESSING ROOM - DAY   121

       Sheryl and Dwayne stare at each other. Dwayne tries to push
       past. Sheryl stops him.

                          DWAYNE
                   I'm gonna tell her.

                          SHERYL
                   Wait. Listen to me.
                       (teary-eyed)
                   Olive is who she is. This is what she's
                   chosen to do...

122   INT. OLIVE'S STATION - DAY   122

       Olive turns, walks mechanically back to her chair and sits.

                          SHERYL (O.S.)
                   ...She's worked hard, she's poured
                   herself into it...

123   INT. PAGEANT DRESSING ROOM - DAY   123

       Sheryl puts a hand on Dwayne's shoulder.

                          SHERYL
                   ...We can't take it away from her.
                   We just can't.

       Dwayne closes his eyes, hangs his head. Sheryl hugs him.

                          SHERYL (cont'd)
                   I know you want to protect her,
                   but... We gotta let Olive be
                   Olive. For better or worse...

       Pam, the clipboard-wielding Assistant returns.

                          PAM
                   Olive Hoover? Are you the family?

       They nod and return -- en masse -- to the dressing room.

124   INT. OLIVE'S STATION - DAY   124

       Olive is seated in her chair, staring dumbly at the floor.

                    SHERYL
          Olive? Time to go.

Olive doesn't move. Sheryl goes to her.

                    SHERYL (cont'd)
          Olive...? Honey, are you okay?

Olive won't look at her. Sheryl glances at Richard.

                    PAM
          Um... We need to go.

                    SHERYL
          Hang on.
                    (to Olive)
          Honey...? Olive, look at me.
                    (Olive looks)
          You don't have to do this if you
          don't want. If you want to sit
          this one out, that's fine. We're
          proud of you anyway, okay?

A beat. Pam checks her watch.

                    PAM
          It's time.

Silence.

Olive stands up. She walks to the Assistant.

                    PAM (cont'd)
          Okay. Let's go.

She takes Olive's hand. They stride off. Dwayne, Sheryl, and
Richard stand and watch -- powerless -- as Olive is led off.

124A INT. HOTEL HALLWAY - DAY   124A

TRACKING BACKWARDS with Olive. She's got her game face on --
a mask of fear and determination. Sheryl calls after her.

                    SHERYL
          Good luck, honey!

Olive keeps walking.

124B INT. BACKSTAGE HALLWAY - DAY   124B

Olive is led down a long industrial hallway.

125   INT. REGISTRATION HALL - DAY   125

       Frank re-enters. Dwayne, Sheryl, and Richard are coming the
       other way.

                       FRANK
            Is she going on?

                      DWAYNE
            She's going on.

       They enter the auditorium together.

126   INT. AUDITORIUM - NIGHT   126

       Yet another LITTLE BLOND GIRL is on stage, taking her bows to
       polite APPLAUSE. Richard leads Sheryl, Dwayne, and Frank to
       their seats. The MC comes on stage.

                       MC
            Very nice. Thank you. Okay, you've been
            a patient audience tonight...

       IN THE WINGS

       Olive stands next to the edge of the curtain watching the MC.

                       MC (cont'd)
            ...We have one more contestant and then
            we'll be crowning the winner. So please
            welcome, from Laguna Beach, Olive Hoover!

       APPLAUSE.

       WE FOLLOW Olive out onto the stage.

       The LIGHTS are blinding.

       The AUDIENCE is hidden in darkness.

       There's a crowd MURMUR because of her hot-pants get-up.

       Dwayne, Frank, Sheryl, and Richard applaud nervously.

       Richard takes Sheryl's hand, squeezes it. They share a look.

       Olive waves over the MC. He walks over to her and holds the
       mic down for her to speak. She takes a breath.

                       OLIVE
            I'd like to dedicate this to my
            Grandpa, who helped me do this
            routine.

                         MC
          That's sweet! Is he here? Where's
          your Grandpa right now?

                       OLIVE
          He's in the trunk of our car.

The MC doesn't know how to react.

                         MC
          Okay! Well! Take it away, Olive!

He retreats. She is alone on stage. Some 12 YEAR OLD BOYS
in the audience decide to be cruel. One of them "moos".

                      BOY ONE
          Moooo!

GIGGLES and SHUSHES. Another boy chimes in.

                      BOY TWO
          Arf! Arf! Arf!

More GIGGLES and SHUSHES. Miss California, at the judges
table by the stage, looks around sternly. She feels bad for
Olive.

Olive is confused. She doesn't understand these noises.

Dwayne hangs his head. Frank looks around.

                       FRANK
          Where are those fuckers?! I'll
          kill 'em!

Then Olive finds what she's looking for:

Kirby, in the sound booth.

He nods at her.

She nods at him.

Then Olive turns around, her back to the audience.

Kirby turns a VOLUME knob up to "6". He hits "play".

A BLAST of hard rock 12 bar blues comes out of the speakers.

Everyone is surprised.

The music is hard-driving and nasty. It is <u>completely
different</u> from the other pageant music we've heard.

For the first four measures, Olive barely moves, rocking her shoulders and hips to the beat.

Dwayne, Frank, Sheryl, and Richard all glance at each other.

This is not what they expected.

No one knows what to make of Olive rocking, her back turned.

However, when the first verse begins, Olive turns and strides up the stage -- hands on hips, shoulders swinging -- with an absolute and spectacular physical self-confidence.

She rocks out, busting crazy moves this stage has never seen: shakes, shimmies, twirls, dips, undulations -- a melange of MTV rump-shakin', Solid Gold Dancers re-runs, and out-of-left-field inventions of her own. Other moves are clearly drawn from Grandpa's sixty-year career of strip-bar patronage.

She dances with a total command -- an exuberant, even witty mastery of her body, the music, the moves, everything.

Most of all, she's doing it for herself -- for her own sense of fun -- and the judges are instantly irrelevant.

The audience is stunned. No one moves. Mouths hang open.

Sheryl, Frank, and Dwayne gape. Richard is baffled.

                         RICHARD
               What's she doing? What the hell is
               she doing?!

When the first verse ends, Olive punctuates the 12-bar vamp with a series of violent pelvic thrusts.

Everyone is totally shocked. No one knows how to react.

                         SHERYL
               Oh, my God...!

Abruptly, Dwayne stands and cheers Olive, pumping his fist to the music -- a lone voice in the wilderness.

Frank -- recognizing absurdity when he sees it -- bursts out laughing. He stands, suddenly exhilarated, and joins Dwayne, cheering, whistling, and trying to get the rest of the crowd into it. Sheryl, relieved and amazed, stands and joins them.

Richard stares at them. Cautiously encouraged, he stands and cheers -- tentative, then more and more unself-consciously.

Grandpa was right -- she's blowing them out of the water.

As the second verse ends and the guitar solo begins, Olive punctuates the vamp with another series of thrusts.

This is too much for Ms. Jenkins -- the Official from the registration desk, who sits near the stage at the table of contest JUDGES, including Miss California. She looks around and spots Sheryl, Richard and Frank standing and cheering.

The Official gets up, walks up the aisle and yells at Sheryl.

                    MS. JENKINS
          What is your daughter doing?!

Sheryl -- taken aback -- has no answer. Richard leans in.

                    RICHARD
          She's kicking ass, is what she's
          doing!

The others smile and nod. The Official is incensed. She turns and walks back to the sound booth. She yells at Kirby.

                    MS. JENKINS
          Turn it off!

                    KIRBY
          What?

                    MS. JENKINS
          Turn the music off!!!

                    KIRBY
                 (fake deaf)
          What...?!

He smiles and cranks the music up to "8". Mothers and children in the audience clap their hands over their ears.

Around the auditorium, confusion reigns. A scattering of people (the Grizzled Biker, Miss California, etc.) stand and cheer Olive on. Others sit dumbfound -- unsure how to react.

Still others frown disapprovingly, shaking their heads. A handful of Moms flee for the exit, hands over their ears.

Ms. Jenkins, furious, leaves Kirby and stalks down the aisle to the stage. Sheryl watches with growing worry.

                    SHERYL
          What's she doing? Look...!

She shakes Richard, points.

Ms. Jenkins goes to the MC -- at the side of the stage -- waves to him. He bends down, listens. He nods.

The MC walks on stage and tries to stop Olive from dancing, grabbing her arms.

Olive doesn't know what he's doing, but she won't let him break her routine. She wiggles away and keeps dancing.

Richard -- outraged -- races to the front of the auditorium, leaps on the stage, jumps on the MC's back and rides him -- piggy-back -- into the wings. They crash to the ground.

Dwayne and Frank immediately follow him up into the wings, instinctively looking to back Richard up.

Olive stops dancing, turns and looks at Richard.

Richard, grappling with the MC, waves her on.

                    RICHARD
          Keep dancing, Honey! Just dance!

Frank and Dwayne gesture too -- keep dancing!

Olive turns and stares at the audience.

Sheryl gestures -- "Keep going!"

Olive -- hearing the music, seeing Sheryl -- nods her head to the music and starts to dance again, fluid and relaxed.

Richard is pulled off the pissed-off MC by two HOTEL SECURITY GUARDS who step in and pull them apart. Richard shrugs off their restraining hands, then turns to watch Olive dance.

Ms. Jenkins steps forward and angrily confronts him.

                    MS. JENKINS
          Get your daughter off stage now!

Richard -- taken aback -- hesitates. She presses.

                    MS. JENKINS (cont'd)
          If you don't stop her, she'll be
          disqualified!

Richard stares. Then he nods.

                    RICHARD
          Okay.

He turns and walks out on stage.

Olive, seeing him, is confused. He steps up behind her.

Then -- in sync with Olive -- Richard starts dancing.

They dance together: Olive in front, Richard backing her up.

Richard looks at Ms. Jenkins with a defiant, fuck-you smile.

Frank and Dwayne, watching, can't believe it.

                    DWAYNE
          Holy shit...!

Sheryl shakes her head -- she can't believe it either.

Frank steps out on stage, and dances next to Richard -- a
surprisingly competent set of butt-wagging, party-music
moves. Dwayne follows Frank, rockin' out as best he can.

Sheryl pauses a moment and watches her family.

Richard waves to Sheryl to join them.

A beat. Sheryl walks, then runs, and jumps up on stage.

Richard helps her up, and they dance together.

Kirby cranks it to "10". MUSIC is overpowering everything.

As the songs winds up, Sheryl, Richard, Frank and Dwayne line
up next to Olive for a unified series of thrusts.

A few audience MEMBERS respond with a standing ovation.

Frank and Dwayne strut around with their arms in the air,
like victorious professional wrestlers.

Richard picks up Olive, swings her in the air.

Sheryl walks over and hugs Richard and Olive.

                              FADE TO BLACK AND SILENCE

127 INT. OFFICE - NIGHT   127

Richard, Sheryl, Olive, Frank, and Dwayne sit -- dazed -- in
a drab office. They're handcuffed together, except Olive.

Boxes of pageant materials -- trophies, sashes, tiaras -- are
stacked around them.

Nothing's happening. Florescent lights HUM.

Frank and Dwayne are still wearing their "LOSER" T-shirts.

Sheryl quietly eyes Richard, slouched next to her, and smiles
to herself. Her eyes drift to a nearby carton of tiaras.

A door OPENS. They all look over. A cop -- Officer Martinez
-- appears, starts taking off their handcuffs.

                    OFFICER MARTINEZ
          Okay. You're out.

                    RICHARD
          We're free?

                    OFFICER MARTINEZ
          They're dropping charges. On the
          condition that you don't enter your
          child in a beauty contest in the
          State of California ever again.

                    FRANK
               (hesitates)
          I think we can live with that.

128 INT. REGISTRATION HALL - NIGHT   128

Richard, Sheryl, Olive, Frank, and Dwayne step into the
lobby. It's deserted. Decorations and banners litter the
floor. They wander out, dazed, rubbing their wrists.

Sheryl approaches Richard, takes a tiara from behind her
back, places it on his head. Richard accepts it wryly.

                    RICHARD
          Great. Thank you very much.

She smiles. Richard turns to Olive with the tiara.

                    RICHARD (cont'd)
          Here. I think this is for you.

                    OLIVE
          Dad...!

She struggles to articulate something. Finally, she shrugs.

                    OLIVE (cont'd)
          I just like dancing...!

                    RICHARD
          Well, you were great.

                    FRANK
          You were beyond great.

                    DWAYNE
          You were incredible.

                         OLIVE
                    (shy)
              Thank you.

They all smile at her. Then Richard looks around.

                         RICHARD
              Let's get the fuck out of here...!

                                              CUT TO BLACK

SOUNDS of cars on a distant highway.

                         RICHARD (V.O.) (cont'd)
              ...So it's two in the morning...

129 EXT. REST STOP - DAY   129

     Everyone is seated at a picnic table at a road-side rest
     stop. Cars WHIZZ by on a highway in the far background.

     They've finished eating -- an empty bucket of KFC and bottles
     of Diet Sprite litter the table. Richard is telling a story.

     Everyone is relaxed -- smiling and listening.

                         RICHARD
              ...He's in this dumpster behind the
              racetrack... And it starts to rain.
                    (laughter)
              He's crawling around, cursing like
              a pirate, looking for this ticket I
              threw away. Suddenly he goes,
              "Richard, don't drop the light!" I
              go, "Don't what?" He goes, "Drop
              the fucking light!" So I go...
                    (mimes dropping light)
              Right in the water! He's like...
                    (mimes electric shock)
              Ahhhaahhhaahhhaahhhhhh!!!
                    (appalled laughter)
              I pull the light out -- he's lying
              there, rain is pouring down... And
              he's got the ticket! This twelve
              hundred dollar trifecta! I'm like,
              "Dad, are you okay?" He looks at
              me and all he says is: "Richard...
              Don't ever have children."

     Everyone bursts out laughing.

                         RICHARD (cont'd)
              To me, he says that! To me!

     The mirth tapers off. They glance at each other.

Frank holds up his bottle of Diet Sprite.

                    FRANK
          Here's to Grandpa.

                    EVERYONE
          Here's to Grandpa.

They clink and drink. Richard nods to a snack shack nearby.

                    RICHARD
          So... Who wants some ice-cream?

                                        CUT TO BLACK

                    THE END

SCENE NOTES

I have slightly more than 100 drafts of *Little Miss Sunshine* in my computer. None of them, however, could be said to represent the definitive version. A script is always just a continuing series of revisions, and any one draft represents a mere snapshot of an ongoing process.

I've chosen the June 6, 2005, draft to be published because that was the first day of principal photography—the moment, figuratively speaking, when I passed the baton to the film's directors, Jonathan Dayton and Valerie Faris.

Scripts are sometimes compared to blueprints, but that analogy—to my mind—makes the transition from page to screen seem dry and overdetermined. A better metaphor might be a recipe, which allows for a sense of variation, improvisation, and collaboration among partners.

I have been—I admit freely—the luckiest screenwriter in the world, having been blessed with some of the smartest and most generous collaborators a writer could hope for. The film is a beautiful elaboration of the screenplay by a number of supremely talented individuals—producers, directors, cast, and crew—and I've tried to note some of their specific contributions in the pages below.

Scene 12: The call from Cindy is the story's inciting incident, and in the early drafts of the script I thought showing the call come in to the empty Hoover kitchen might help hook the audience into the story. It was one of those ideas that was put into the script and taken out several times.

This version of the script was actually shot. The directors, Jonathan and Valerie, had the camera do a long, slow 360-degree pan of the Hoover household while the message was received. In the end, Jon and Val decided to cut Cindy's call in the interest of pacing.

Scene 15: Frank and Dwayne's first exchange is a little longer here than in the film. Jon and Val, the directors, wisely cut it down to its bare bones.

This is something that happened often—small flourishes that read well on the page were cut in order to keep the story moving forward. This is perhaps the biggest lesson I learned in seeing the movie get made: simpler is better. Make your point and move on.

Scene 21: In the film, Richard tries to talk to Sheryl while she is on the phone with Cindy ("They have to . . . ! They have to!"). All of those lines were improvisations by Greg Kinnear, who was tireless in his efforts to help make the film better than the script. His performance in this scene is a great example of an actor taking nothing (on the page) and turning it into something real and wonderful.

Scene 26: Richard's speech to Olive ("There's no sense in entering a contest if you don't think you're gonna win") is a crucial plot point—the hero's (Richard's) flawed reaction to the story's inciting incident (Aunt Cindy's call).

Had Richard responded to the call in a healthy way ("It's okay if you win, it's okay if you lose; let's just go have fun!"), there would be no story. Making Olive promise she'll win the Little Miss Sunshine pageant sets up a ticking time bomb that will detonate in the story's climax.

I am only now, after years of writing, starting to realize how crucial this specific plot point—the hero's flawed reaction to the inciting incident—is to story construction in general. It goes to show how you can write for years and still feel like a beginner.

Scene 27: The scene of Sheryl putting Grandpa to bed was shot but, again, cut in the interest of speed and pacing.

Scene 28: This is a scene that almost didn't make it into the movie, as several people felt it slowed the story down too much. To me, though, the first night Frank and Dwayne spend together was just too strange and wonderful to skip over. Jonathan and Valerie agreed with me, and together we were able to keep the scene on the shooting schedule.

Scene 29: Grandpa's conversation with Frank about Sunset Manor ("I know you're a homo but maybe you can appreciate this") was cut at the last minute in an effort to lower the script's page count. Jon and Val snuck those pages back into the script after shooting began, and they made it into the final cut. Thank you, Jon and Val.

Scene 30: This scene, in the diner, never really had a button at the end. Having Dwayne blow his straw wrapper at Richard was something Paul Dano came up with in rehearsals, and Jon and Val incorporated it into the shoot. Thank you, Paul.

Scene 32: In the film, Sheryl echoes Richard's instructions back to him: "Push it hard." That line is pure Toni Collette.
Thank you, Toni.

Scene 34: This scene was not in the original script, but got added in the course of development in an effort to add depth to Sheryl's story and background. Unfortunately, this kind of scene—exposition for exposition's sake—tends to stick out. It ended up being cut.

Scene 35: An example of me overwriting. In the film, Richard asks, "There's no hill. How do we . . . ?" and the Mechanic just looks at them and smiles. Cut to the family pushing the bus.
In the script, I have the Mechanic explain the whole bus-pushing idea. Fortunately, that redundant bit of dialogue (and many others) ended up on the cutting room floor.

Scene 37: My favorite bit of dialogue is, alas, not in the script. When Grandpa asks Olive, "Was that fun?" that moment is a pure, spontaneous Alan Arkin improv. Thank you, Alan.

Scene 40: In the film, Frank's hilarious responses to Grandpa's request for porn ("All righty . . . ! I will . . . !") came entirely from Steve Carell. Thank you, Steve.

Scene 47: This scene was omitted for budget reasons. Here it is, in its entirety:

INT. MCDONALDS – NIGHT
Everyone sits at a table eating. No one says anything.

Scene 53: This scene was filmed on the last day of the shoot. Alan Arkin had long felt this scene—as written—was a little too sweet and made Grandpa a bit too cuddly just before his final exit. He asked me to come up with something rougher and saltier for Grandpa to say to Olive. I wrote a couple of versions of the scene, but nothing quite hit the mark for him. Then Alan asked if he could try writing some of his own lines and I—no fool—said yes. The result is some of the most beloved dialogue in the film. So, credit where credit is due. Thank you, Alan.

Scene 54: Jonathan and Valerie moved this short scene to another place in the film, tying it to Sheryl's cigarette break.

Scene 55: This is a big one: Sheryl proposes a trial separation to Richard. I was always cognizant of the fact that Sheryl had a much shallower arc than the other characters. I wanted to deepen her story, but at the same time was afraid of piling too much drama into a single weekend. I put this line in the script, but was always ambivalent about it. It was shot, but subsequently cut by Jon and Val. I don't miss it.

Scene 68: Another example of overwriting. Sheryl alludes to the possibility of bankruptcy in her family meeting with Olive and Dwayne. It makes Sheryl's speech way too long and was, thankfully, cut from the film.

Dwayne's view out the window is one of several POV shots I wrote into the script. None of them, I believe, were filmed. The lesson here is that you direct a film with a camera, not a typewriter.

Scene 72: In the original script, Richard peered out a third-floor window. Thankfully, Jonathan and Valerie talked me into changing it to a ground-floor window.

Scene 73: In every draft of the script, I ended this scene with a hard cut from Richard's speech, thinking that was funny.

The way it works in the film, though—with Sheryl agreeing to Richard's plan and saying, "Let's do it"—is infinitely better. Seeing Sheryl make that decision gives the audience permission to go along with this farcical development and (for most people) keeps the thread of believability intact. This change came entirely from the directors, Jon and Val. While there are scores of moments in the film where Jonathan and Valerie's direction improved upon the writing, this is—to me—the most emblematic. They dialed back the comedy and simply made the scene as real as possible.

Scene 75: I kind of miss this little exchange between Olive and Sheryl about Grandpa's soul being in Heaven. I don't know why it got cut from the movie, and I never had the courage to ask Jon and Val about it. Too sentimental, I suspect.

Scene 80: The State Trooper scene was something I was always on the fence about. It's the one scene in the movie that doesn't need to be there—it exists solely to lighten the mood after Grandpa's death. Since Dwayne's freakout is about to happen, I wanted to give the audience a bit of comic relief. I never dreamed it would play as well as it does.

Much of the scene's success is owed to the inspired improvisations of Greg Kinnear. "The Sweet Sweetness" was a phrase that caught on in the film's editing suites and became the name of the film's postproduction newsletter.

Scene 89: This is the race-to-the-hotel sequence as it was originally written. In the course of preproduction, the film's location scouts found a hotel in Long Beach, just off the 405 freeway, that matched almost perfectly the location described in the script. Permission from the city was secured and the shoot was scheduled for that location.

In the midst of production, however, the city of Long Beach withdrew its permission for shooting at that location. We had to scramble to find a new location on short notice, and ended up with a hotel in Ventura. I had to rewrite the script to accommodate the new location. I prefer this version.

Scene 101: Richard's final pep talk with Olive is a perfect example of a writer—me—trying too hard to spell things out. The scene was shot but, thankfully, cut from the movie.

Scene 104: The Biker Dad is just that, a Biker Dad. Nothing more.

Scenes 105, 107, and 112: In the original script, the family traveled from suburban Maryland to Boca Raton, Florida.

I wrote this sequence—the Surfboard Scene—while imagining the clear, turquoise waters of the Florida coast. In the five years that the script bounced around Hollywood, a number of people told me that this scene—of baptism and rebirth in the ocean—was their favorite scene in the script. Such was my attachment to it that when the location of the movie was changed to California (for budget reasons), I clung steadfastly to my original vision.

Thus, on June 23, 2005, Paul Dano and Steve Carell spent an entire day in the cold, murky waters off Malibu, floating on surfboards and trying to have a conversation about Proust. It was, needless to say, a disaster. The full day of shooting was scrapped, and the entire scene was later reshot on a pier in Ventura. In the movie, it works beautifully.

This was a lesson in the virtues of simplicity. While the sequence in my head was lovely (it originally included underwater shots of Frank and Dwayne swimming through shafts of sunlight, over shimmering white sand), it was never going to be made on a low budget.

The scene was, essentially, a conversation about Proust. Anything that distracted from that (say, the ocean) was superfluous and should have been cut from the script.

Scene 114: I had misgivings about this scene as the film went into production. Now it makes me cringe. The script was written in 2000, when Loser Chic was not quite yet a cliché. By 2005, it was a cliché. Thankfully, this scene was cut.

Scene 119: This scene, in which Richard explains why he doesn't want Olive to perform, is obviously overwritten.

In the original script, Richard never went backstage—only Dwayne tried to rescue Olive. While the film was in development, however, countless hours were spent trying to clarify the arc of Richard's character. It was thought that sending Richard backstage to express some doubt and humility would make him a more sympathetic character.

This was true, but you don't need a big speech to do it. All you need is the line, "I don't want her to go on." A great actor like Greg will do the rest nonverbally.

I've decided, though, that there's no "right" way to write a scene like this. You can never be sure if you're being too subtle or too obvious until you've shot the scene and cut it together. It seems prudent, then, to err on the side of obviousness—to write the scene "fat"—and then try to find the right balance in the editing room. Again, thank you, Jon and Val.

Scene 124B: "Twenty-five is performance-ready and we're walking . . ."
Thank you, Mary Lynn Rajskub.

Scene 126: I spent five years worrying about the final dance scene of *Little Miss Sunshine*. If it didn't work, the whole film would fail. I spent hours talking with Jonathan and Valerie about what kind of music Olive should be dancing to (originally it was "Peach" by Prince) and what kind of moves she should be doing.

When the film went into production, I was sorely tempted to impose myself on the dance rehearsals and dictate exactly how Olive's choreography should proceed. Fortunately, sanity prevailed and I restrained myself.

It was the film's choreographer, Marguerite Derricks, who first proposed that Olive's dance be a striptease. It seems obvious in retrospect, but at the time it was like a magic bullet. Olive didn't have to be a great dancer—she could be clunky as hell—as long as she was having fun.

Thank you, Marguerite.

Scene 129: This scene was shot as written, and it didn't work at all. It was far too long, and it made the Hoover family too happy, too healed, too reconciled with each other.

Six weeks before Sundance, I wrote the ending that appears in the film. It was shot in a single day in Ventura.

—Michael Arndt

HOW TO WRITE A SUNDANCE HIT IN NINE EASY STEPS

Since the release of *Little Miss Sunshine,* I am often accosted by strangers—many of them aspiring screenwriters—who demand to know how I was able to write a film that earned standing ovations at the Sundance Film Festival and won critical and commercial success. "It was easy," I say.

I have, in fact, distilled the lessons of my labor into a simple nine-step program that will allow anyone—even you!—to write the next Sundance hit.

Step 1. Be Unrealistic.

Only a madman would sit down to write a script believing it will one day become a successful movie. Be a madman. As the Book of the Samurai notes, "Nothing great ever came from common sense. One must become insane and desperate."

Step 2. Fail Repeatedly.

Without going into unseemly detail, suffice to say I was no stranger to disappointment when I sat down to write LMS.

Step 3. Choose a Subject That Inspires Widespread Revulsion.

While a small-but-passionate minority of the public will line up on Friday night to see a movie about child beauty pageants, most will not. By cleverly choosing a premise guaranteed to alienate nearly everyone, I had the entire child-beauty-pageant-comedy genre to myself.

Step 4. Procrastinate.

Having settled upon one of the least commercial premises in the history of cinema, I postponed any labor on it for several years, allowing the story to ripen in my mind. When I finally sat down to write the script, in May of 2000, I finished a first draft in three days.

Step 5. Don't Trust Yourself.

This is key. Writers must believe in themselves creatively, but we are uniquely ill-equipped to judge our own work. Let someone else tell you when it's finished.

Step 6. Be a Coward.

I wrote LMS with the intention of directing it. When my agent, in our first phone call, told me this would make it harder to sell, it took me less than a second to throw my cherished ambitions out the window. "But I don't have to!" I blurted. *Little Miss Sunshine* was subsequently directed by Jonathan Dayton and Valerie Faris, who made a far better film than I ever could have.

Step 7. Get Fired.

In 2002, the project was acquired by a studio, Focus Features. I fought bravely to preserve the integrity of my vision by refusing to make wholesale changes to the script. I was quickly fired and replaced by another writer. Luckily, he was fired too. Then the head of the studio was fired. Then I was rehired. After that, I did whatever they wanted.

Step 8. Give Up.

In late 2004, after two years in development, Focus put the project into turnaround. I gave up. *Little Miss Sunshine,* I realized, would never be made.

Fortunately, one of the film's producers, Marc Turtletaub, is not merely one of the handsomest, wittiest, and most intelligent men in Hollywood— he is also a man of great resourcefulness. A month later, we had a "go" picture.

Step 9. Pretend You Knew What You Were Doing.

Talent—they say—will only get you so far, as will persistence, intelligence, determination, and grit. None of these qualities, however, holds a candle to the power of sheer dumb luck. My story is proof of that.

—Michael Arndt

ACKNOWLEDGMENTS

In her 1968 essay, "Trash, Art, and the Movies," Pauline Kael wrote:

> A good movie can take you out of your dull funk and . . .
> make you feel alive again. . . . Good movies make you care, make
> you believe in possibilities again. If somewhere in the
> Hollywood-entertainment world someone has managed to break
> through with something that speaks to you, then it isn't all
> corruption. . . . The world makes a little bit of sense. Sitting there
> alone . . . you know there must be others perhaps in this very
> theater . . . who react as you do.

Movies are, in the end, a form of communication. Every filmgoer knows the thrill of finding on-screen "something that speaks to you"; something that cuts through the fog of everyday life and offers the reassurance that someone, somewhere, sees the world as you do.

The equation works both ways. Writing a script is an attempt to communicate something that can't be communicated otherwise. A screenwriter sends his or her script out like a message in a bottle, hoping beyond rational hope that it might, against all odds, engender a sympathetic response. In this respect, I have been blessed beyond measure.

Three people—my brother David, and my friends Justin Dorazio and Karyn Kusama—were the core reading group that suffered through every draft and slowly, with infinite patience, helped make the script better.

My agents, Bill Weinstein and Tom Strickler, believed in the script from the very beginning and stuck with it through five years of sometimes torturous development.

Jennifer Fox, an early supporter, spent six weeks in the autumn of 2001 gently pushing me to clarify each character arc and encouraging me to sprinkle the story with the small details that bring a script to life.

Marc Turtletaub, David Friendly, Albert Berger, Ron Yerxa, Peter Saraf, and Jeb Brody all contributed equally to producing *Little Miss Sunshine*. Marc, however, must be acknowledged as first among equals—without him, the film wouldn't exist.

Jonathan Dayton and Valerie Faris deserve my undying gratitude. No one did more to shape and improve the script than they did, and their unfailing warmth and good humor make it difficult, at times, to believe that they really are Hollywood directors.

Alan Arkin, Abigail Breslin, Steve Carell, Toni Collette, Paul Dano, and Greg Kinnear exceeded every expectation I had in bringing the Hoover family to life. Their contributions to the script have been duly noted.

I'm thankful to each and every member of the LMS cast and crew, whose contributions—if enumerated—could fill an entire book.

And I'm grateful to Peter Rice and the team at Fox Searchlight for their perspicacious and enthusiastic support of the movie.

Finally, I'm grateful—more than you can imagine—to you, the movie-goer/script reader, for your interest in my script and the movie it turned into. You've made my world a bit less lonely, and I can only hope I've been able to return the favor. Thank you.

—Michael Arndt
San Francisco
12:07 a.m., November 6, 2006

CAST AND CREW CREDITS

FOX SEARCHLIGHT PICTURES
In association with Big Beach
Present
A Dayton/Faris Film
A Big Beach/Bona Fide Production

"LITTLE MISS SUNSHINE"

GREG KINNEAR   TONI COLLETTE   STEVE CARELL   PAUL DANO
with ABIGAIL BRESLIN and ALAN ARKIN

Directed by
JONATHAN DAYTON &
VALERIE FARIS

Written by
MICHAEL ARNDT

Produced by
MARC TURTLETAUB
DAVID T. FRIENDLY
PETER SARAF
ALBERT BERGER &
RON YERXA

Executive Producers
JEB BRODY
MICHAEL BEUGG

Director of Photography
TIM SUHRSTEDT, A.S.C.

Production Design by
KALINA IVANOV

Edited by
PAMELA MARTIN

Costumes Designed by
NANCY STEINER

Music Composed by
MYCHAEL DANNA

Featuring Music by
DEVOTCHKA

Music Supervisors
SUSAN JACOBS & ANNE LITT

Casting by
KIM DAVIS-WAGNER
& JUSTINE BADDELEY

Unit Production Manager
MICHAEL BEUGG

First Assistant Director
THOMAS PATRICK SMITH

Second Assistant Director
GREGORY SMITH

Choreography by
MARGUERITE DERRICKS

CAST
(In order of appearance)

Olive . . . . Abigail Breslin
Richard . . . . Greg Kinnear
Dwayne . . . . Paul Dano
Grandpa . . . . Alan Arkin
Sheryl . . . . Toni Collette
Frank . . . . Steve Carell
Doctor #1 . . . . Marc Turtletaub
Cindy . . . . Jill Talley
Diner Waitress . . . . Brenda Canela
Mechanic . . . . Julio Oscar Mechoso
Convenience Store
Proprietor . . . . Chuck Loring
Josh . . . . Justin Shilton
Larry Sugarman . . . . . Gordon Thomson
Teen Boy #1 . . . Steven Christopher Parker
Stan Grossman . . . . Bryan Cranston
Doctor #2 . . . . John Walcutt
Linda . . . . Paula Newsome
State Trooper McCleary . . . . Dean Norris
Pageant Official Jenkins . . . . . Beth Grant

Kirby . . . . Wallace Langham
Miss California . . . . . . Lauren Shiohama
Pageant Assistant Pam . . Mary Lynn Rajskub
Funeral Home Worker . . . . . . Jerry Giles
Biker Dad . . . . Geoff Meed
Pageant MC . . . . Matt Winston
Judge . . . . Joan Scheckel
Girl in Hallway . . . . Casandra Ashe
Officer Martinez . . . . Mel Rodriguez

Pageant Contestants
Alexandria Alaman   Alissa Anderegg
Brittany Baird   Cambria Baird
Brenae Bandy   Kristen Holaas
Maliah Hudson   Destry Jacobs
Lindsey Jordan   Shane Murphy
Annabelle Roberts   Sydni Stevenson-Love
Nicole Stoehr   Lauren Yee

Stunt Coordinator . . Tom Robinson Harper
Assistant Stunt
Coordinator . . . . Kenny Anderson

Stunt Players

Christie Abercrombie	Kacie Borrowman
Clay Boss	Peter C. Cullen
Rick Gunderson	Riley Thomas Harper
Johnny Johnson	Matt Taylor
Tim Trella	

"Richard" Stand In . . . Joe Everett Michaels
"Frank" Stand In . . . . Kevin Maier
"Sheryl" Stand In . . . . . Jenny Worman
"Olive" Stand In. . Tracie Richelle Harrison

CREW

Production Supervisor . . . Bob Dohrmann
Location Manager. . . . . . . Chris Miller
Associate Producer. . . . . . . Bart Lipton
Art Director . . . . Alan E. Muraoka
Set Decorator . . . . . . Melissa Levander
Art Department
Coordinator . . . . Theresa Greene
A Camera Operator . . . . Jeffrey P. Greeley
Steadicam Operator/B Camera
Operator. . . . . . . Larry "Doc" Karman
First Assistant Camera . . . Theda Streetman
Heather Lea
Second Assistant
Camera. . . . . . . Gregory H. Dellerson
Rigney Sackley
Film Loader. . . . . Michelle Pizanis
Script Supervisors . . . Lyn Matsuda-Norton
Suzanne C. Swindle
Sound Mixer . . . Steven A. Morrow, C.A.S.
Boom Operator . . . . . . Craig Dollinger
Cable Person . . . . Robert Sharman
Video Assist. . . . . Ed Casares
24 Frame Playback. . . . . Dan Murbarger
Gaffer. . . . . Paul W. McIlvaine
Best Boy Electric . . . . . Matthew Bardocz
Electricians . . . . Keith Hascher
Alan "Monk" Morier
Brian Cantrell
Russell Curtis
Steve Rollins
Key Grip . . . . Paul H. Goodstein
Best Boy Grip . . . . Chris Rossi
Dolly Grip . . . . . . Carlos M. Gallardo
Grips. . . . . Clint J. Borden
Josh Denering
Aaron Vyvial
Rick Lawrence
Assistant Location Manager . . . Nate Taylor
Location Scout. . . . . Dan Milner
Property Master. . . . . . Tony Bonaventura

Assistant Property Master . . . Ellis Barbacoff
Additional Props . . . . Jenn Baum
Andrea Cantrell
Lead Scenic Artist . . . . Troy Hope
Lead Person . . . . . Michael Klingerman
Set Dressing Buyer . . . . Jill Deibler
Set Dressers . . . . Rion Waller
Joe Garcia
David Marple
On-Set Dresser . . . . Chris Pappas
Costume Supervisor. . . . Robin McMullan
Key Costumer . . . . Jennifer Starzyk
Costumer . . . . Lisa Hyde
Department Head Makeup . . Torsten Witte
Key Makeup. . . . . Angel Radefeld
Makeup Assistant . . . . . Nicole Sortillion
Department Head Hair . . . . . Janis Clark
Key Hair Stylists . . . . Susan Carol-Schwary
"Dugg" Kirkpatrick
Casting Associate . . . . Cate Engel
Casting Assistant . . . . . Yasmin Redoblado
Extras Casting. . . . . Rich King
Kelly Hunt
Production Coordinator
. . . . Michyl-Shannon Quilty
Assistant Production Coordinator
. . . . Charissa Deann McLain
Second Second Assistant Director
. . . . Kate Greenberg
Additional 2nd 2nd Assistant Directors
. . . . Heather Anderson
Joe May
Office Production Assistants
. . . . Francis Hadinoto
Joshua Mandel
Jason Mandel

Set Production Assistants

Paul Young	Christopher Licata
Liron Reiter	Negar Saddigh
Rocsana Saddigh	Katherine A. Taylor

Big Beach Production Executive
. . . . Sara Pollack
Assistant to Ms. Collette . . . . . Jessica Otto
Assistants to Mr. Dayton & Ms. Faris
. . . . James Kaplan
Joe Lewis
Assistants to Producers . . . Molly Cooper
Felipe Linz
Emily McMaster
Cori Uchida
Production Legal . . . . . . Sloss Law Office
Jacqueline Eckhouse, Esq.
Alison Hunter, Esq.

Distribution Advisory Services
. . . . Cinetic Media
Unit Publicity . . . . Insignia Inc.
Erik Bright
Jesse Salka
Clearance Coordinator . . . . Ashley Kravitz
Still Photographer . . . . Eric Lee
Medic . . . . Mike Artino
Big Beach Finance Executive
. . . . Jennifer Freed
Production Accountant . . . . Mike Revell
First Assistant Accountant . . Bryan Yaconelli
Payroll Accountant . . . . Thomas Farr
Assistant Choreographer . . Jennifer Hamilton
Studio Teachers . . . . . Cecilia M. Cardwell
Christine Miller
Pageant Consultant . . . . . . Rita Alaman
Pageant Coordinators . . . . Andrea McLaws
Teresea Yee
Marcy Stoehr
Faride Gonzalez
Leroy Alaman
Transportation Coordinator . . . Geno Hart
Transportation Captain . . . Adam Pinkstaff
Transportation Co-Captain . . Angel DeSanti
Camera Car & Process Trailer
. . . . Carpenter Camera Cars
Shotmaker
Camera Cars Unlimited
Caterer . . . . Eclipse Catering, Inc.
Chef . . . . Laurent Marchand
Key Craft Service . . . . . . Richard Cody
Craft Service Assistant . . . . . Eric Armao
Assistant Editor . . . . Terel Gibson
Post Production Consulting by EPC
. . . . Joe Fineman
Post Production Supervisor . . Michael Toji
Editorial Intern . . . . . Alex Turtletaub
Post Production Accountant . . Trevanna Post
Sound Editorial Provided by . . . Soundelux
Supervising Sound Editors
. . . . . . Andrew DeCristofaro, M.P.S.E.
Stephen P. Robinson
Assistant Sound Editor . . . . Patrick Cusack
Dialogue Editor . . John C. Stuver, M.P.S.E.
ADR Editor . . Nancy Kyong Nugent, M.P.S.E.
Sound Effects Editor . . . . Steven F. Nelson
Foley Editor . . . . . . Kerry Ann Carmean
ADR Mixers . . . . Ron Bedrosian
Bob Deschaine, CAS
Greg Steele
Foley Mixer . . . . Lucy Sustar
Foley Artists . . . . Greg Barbanell
Diane Marshall

Voice Casting . . . . Barbara Harris
Re-Recording Mixers . . . . . . Rick Ash
Terry Rodman
Mix Technician . . . . Chris Sidor
Re-Recorded at
. . . . Todd-AO Vine Street Studios
Music Editor . . . . Josh Winget
Music Recorded and Mixed by . . . . Brad
Haehnel, Paramount Recording Studios
Additional Performance Music by
. . . . Tony Tisdale

Score Recorded by
DeVotchka
Guitars, Whistles, Piano, Organ
. . . . Nick Urata
Violin, Accordion, Piano
. . . . Thomas Hagerman
Double Bass, Tuba . . . . . . Jeanie Schroder
Drums, Percussion,
Trumpet, Glockenspiel . . . . . Shawn King

Additional Musicians
Cello . . . . John Krovoza
Piano . . . . Mychael Danna

Color Timer . . . . Lee Wimer
Negative Cutter . . Magic Film & Video Works
Dolby Sound Consultant . . . . Bryan Arenas
Video Dailies . . Global Entertainment Partners
Payroll Company . . Entertainment Partners
Production Insurance . . AON/Alfred G. Ruben
Titles and Opticals . . . . Title House Digital
Main Title Design . . . . Pacific Title
Digital Visual Effects . . . . Look Effects Inc.
Visual Effects Supervisor . . . Adam Avitabile
Visual Effects Producer . . . . . Josh Comen

Songs
CHICAGO
Written by Sufjan Stevens
Performed by Sufjan Stevens
Courtesy of Asthmatic Kitty Records

TU ABANDANO
Written by Xocoyotzin Herrera
Performed by Francisco Javier Gonzalez and
Jose Zuniga
Courtesy of LMS Records

ENEMY GUNS
Written by DeVotchKa
Performed by DeVotchKa
Courtesy of Cicero Recordings, LTD.

FIFTEEN YEARS AGO
Written by Raymond A. Smith
Performed by Conway Twitty
Courtesy of Sony / ATV Music Publishing,
L.L.C. dba Tree Productions

LA LLORONA
Traditional
Performed by DeVotchKa
Courtesy of Cicero Recordings, LTD.

MARTINI LOUNGE
Written by David Sparkman,
Scott Nickoley, Jamie Dunlap
Performed by David Sparkman
Courtesy of Marc Ferrari/Master Source

CHANGE THE WORLD
Written by John Ehrlich
Performed by John Ehrlich
Courtesy of Jeco Music

AMERICA THE BEAUTIFUL
Traditional
Arranged by Weba Garretson,
Bob Remstein and Mark Wheaton
Performed by Matt Winston

INFORMATION HIGHWAY
Written by John Ehrlich
Performed by John Ehrlich
Courtesy of Jeco Music

GIVE MY REGARDS
TO BROADWAY
Written by George M. Cohan
Arranged by
Weba Garretson, Bob Remstein
and Mark Wheaton
Performed by Casandra Ashe

YOU'VE GOT ME DANCING
Written By Gordon Pogoda and Barry Upton
Performed By Inspiration
Courtesy of Kid Gloves Music

RODEO QUEEN
Written by Darvin Jordan
Performed by Lindsey Jordan

GIVE IT UP
Written By: Marc Dold and Judith Martin
Performed by Pulse
Courtesy of Kid Gloves Music

LET IT GO
Written by Gordon Pogoda
Performed By Julie Griffin
Courtesy of Kid Gloves Music

SUPER FREAK
Written by Rick James and Alonzo Miller
Performed by Rick James
Courtesy of Motown Records under license
from Universal Music Enterprises
Remix and additional production by
Sebastian Arocha Morton for Rocasound

TIL THE END OF TIME
Written by Nick Urata and DeVotchKa
Performed by DeVotchKa
Produced by Mychael Danna

NO MAN'S LAND
Written by Sufjan Stevens
Performed by Sufjan Stevens
Courtesy of Asthmatic Kitty Records

Special Thanks

Miss America
GotFootage, Inc.
R.P. Productions, Inc.
Body Glove
Converse
Laura Mercier
Murad
Obey
Reebok
Vans

The Filmmakers wish to thank:
The Joan Scheckel Lab
Bob Industries
Mike Mills
Steven Baker
Augusta Dayton
James Dayton
Everett Dayton
Al and Joan Dayton
Jim and Paula Faris
Jocelyn Towne
David Kramer
Warren Dern
Sara Montiel
Maureen Curran
Erika Greene
Sarah Hudnut

Camera Dollies by
J.L. Fisher, Inc.
Chapman/Leonard Studio Equipment, Inc.

Kodak   CFI   Panavision

Dolby   SDDS   DTS

Cinetic

No. 42333
MPAA   IATSE

ABOUT THE FILMMAKERS

JONATHAN DAYTON and VALERIE FARIS (Directors)

Jonathan Dayton and Valerie Faris make their feature film directorial debut with *Little Miss Sunshine*. However, the married team has already built an impressive body of innovative projects as directors and producers in a variety of mediums, collaborating together on over 75 projects in film, television, commercials, and music videos.

Jonathan and Valerie began their careers creating and directing the pioneering MTV show *The Cutting Edge*. They continued to work at the leading edge of music television, directing award-winning videos and documentaries for artists including REM, The Red Hot Chili Peppers, Jane's Addiction, The Smashing Pumpkins, Macy Gray, Janet Jackson, Oasis, Weezer, and The Ramones. Their music productions ultimately earned them two Grammy Awards, nine MTV Music Video Awards, and a Billboard Music "Director of the Year" Award.

In addition, Jonathan and Valerie have worked extensively in television, including directing episodes of the groundbreaking sketch comedy series *Mr. Show with Bob and David* for HBO. They also produced two feature films: the documentary *The Decline of Western Civilization Part II: The Metal Years* for New Line Cinema and Jane's Addiction's *Gift* for Warner Bros. Music.

MICHAEL ARNDT (Writer)

Michael Arndt lives in New York City. *Little Miss Sunshine* is his first produced screenplay.

FOX SEARCHLIGHT PICTURES IN ASSOCIATION WITH BIG BEACH PRESENT A BIG BEACH/BONA FIDE PRODUCTION A JONATHAN DAYTON/VALERIE FARIS FILM 'LITTLE MISS SUNSHINE'
CASTING BY KIM DAVIS-WAGNER AND JUSTINE BADDELEY   COSTUME DESIGN BY NANCY STEINER   MUSIC BY MYCHAEL DANNA   FEATURED MUSIC BY DEVOTCHKA   MUSIC SUPERVISORS SUSAN JACOBS · ANNE LITT   EDITED BY PAMELA MARTIN   PRODUCTION DESIGN BY KALINA IVANOV
DIRECTOR OF PHOTOGRAPHY TIM SUHRSTEDT, ASC   EXECUTIVE PRODUCERS JEB BRODY · MICHAEL BEUGG   PRODUCED BY ALBERT BERGER & RON YERXA AND MARC TURTLETAUB · DAVID T. FRIENDLY · PETER SARAF   WRITTEN BY MICHAEL ARNDT   DIRECTED BY JONATHAN DAYTON AND VALERIE FARIS